BIZARRE CRIMES

BIZARRE CRIMES

Gilda and Melvin Berger

Illustrated by Cheryl Chalmers

Julian Messner New York

Text Copyright © 1984 by Gilda Berger & Melvin Berger

Illustrations Copyright © 1984 by Cheryl Chalmers

All rights reserved including the right of
reproduction in whole or in part in any form.
Published by Julian Messner,
A Division of Simon & Schuster, Inc.
Simon & Schuster Building,
1230 Avenue of the Americas,
New York, New York   10020.
JULIAN MESSNER and colophon are trademarks of
Simon & Schuster, Inc.

Manufactured in the United States of America

Design by Howard B. Petlack, A Good Thing, Inc.

Library of Congress Cataloging in Publication Data.

Berger, Gilda.
  Bizarre crimes.

  Bibliography: p.
  Includes index.
  Summary: Presents ten cases of unusual and daring
crimes involving imposture, swindles, "impossible"
robberies, and complicated confidence games.
    1. Crime and criminals—Biography—Juvenile literature.
[1. Crime and criminals] I. Berger, Melvin. II. Chalmers, Cheryl, ill. III. Title.
HV6245.B45   1984   364.1   84-10750
ISBN 0-671-49371-X

CONTENTS

    INTRODUCTION / **7**
1. / MARTIN GUERRE: AMAZING IMPOSTER / **13**
2. / GENTLEMAN JOE: PRACTICAL JOKER OR SWINDLER? / **20**
3. / VINCENZO PERUGIA: THE THEFT OF THE *MONA LISA* / **29**
4. / ALVES REIS: THE SWINDLER WHO TOPPLED A GOVERNMENT / **37**
5. / SANTA CLAUS: WANTED FOR ROBBERY / **44**
6. / TONY PINO: THE 1950 BRINK'S HOLDUP / **53**
7. / RONALD BIGGS: THE GREAT TRAIN ROBBERY / **61**
8. / CHARLIE MARZANO: THE PUROLATOR HEIST / **68**
9. / FRIC-FRAC: ROBBERY ON THE RIVIERA / **76**
10. / MEL WEINBERG: THE KING OF CON / **85**
    BIBLIOGRAPHY / **92**
    INDEX / **94**

Also by Gilda and Melvin Berger
Bizarre Murders

INTRODUCTION

The thin, dignified-looking man, wearing a lab coat, rushed into Tokyo's Teikdsu Bank just before closing time on January 26, 1948. He had been sent, he said, with medicine that would protect the bank's workers against dysentery, the severe stomach infection that was crippling the city.

The entire staff was brought together in the manager's office. The man in the white coat gave each person a few drops of a liquid to drink. Within minutes, worker after worker fell to the floor, writhing in pain. Twelve died immediately. Three others passed out, but later recovered.

The fake doctor then dashed to the empty tellers' cages, and grabbed nearly 200,000 yen.

The crime was finally traced to Sadamichi Hirasawa, an artist who desperately needed money. The "medicine" was a deadly poison: potassium cyanide. Hirasawa was sentenced to be hanged. However, a series of appeals and stays has kept him on death row. He now has the dubious distinction of being the oldest condemned man in the world.

Alexander T. Stewart was the immensely wealthy owner of New York City's first department store.

He had one main ambition in life: to create a planned city, a City Beautiful he called it, with a giant cathedral at its center. On his death he wished to be buried in the cathedral.

His City Beautiful was built. It is known today as Garden City on Long Island, but it was not completed at the time of Stewart's death in 1876. So his remains were temporarily placed in a crypt—a sealed underground room—in the graveyard of St. Mark's in the Bowery in New York.

Two years later a church sexton discovered that the crypt had been broken open. Thieves had removed the body, along with the silver name plate from the coffin. After a few weeks, his widow received a letter from Canada. The writer offered to return her husband's remains for $200,000. Mrs. Stewart got the price down to $20,000. She also demanded to see the silver name plate as proof that she would be getting her husband's bones.

As soon as the plate arrived, Mrs. Stewart paid the money and received her late husband's remains. By now the Garden City Cathedral was finished. The body was then buried there, according to Mr. Stewart's wishes.

The police tried to find the grave robbers for several years, but the body snatchers were never caught.

"Please throw down the box," the polite bandit said to stagecoach driver John Shine. Shine hesitated. He had never seen such an outlaw. There was a flour sack over his face. On his head was a derby hat. He wore a fancy business suit instead of a traditional cowboy outfit. And he was on foot instead of on horseback.

Noting the pause, robber Black Bart shouted, "If he dares to shoot, give him a solid volley, boys."

Shine turned to see six rifle barrels sticking out of the bushes lining the road. All were aimed straight at him. He threw down the cashbox. Black Bart opened it, scooped up the money, and dashed off into the underbrush.

Shine remained in his seat. He was afraid to move. The six rifles were still pointing at him. After some fifteen minutes, he climbed down. What he saw on the ground amazed him. The six rifles were nothing more than wooden poles balanced on the branches of a bush!

Word of Black Bart's distinctive style spread. He always walked to the scene of his robberies. He wore fancy city clothes, and he spoke softly and politely. In his later robberies, Bart also began to give his victims short poems that he wrote. The following verses are believed to be his:

> Here I lay me down to sleep
> To await the coming morrow.
> Perhaps success, perhaps defeat,
> And everlasting sorrow.

> Let come what will, I'll try it on,
> My condition can't be worse.
> And if there's money in that box
> 'Tis money in my purse.

He signed the poems, "Black Bart, Po-8" (try saying it aloud). The poet, whose real name was

Charles E. Boles, was caught on November 3, 1883, as he attempted his twenty-ninth stagecoach robbery. He was sentenced to ten years at San Quentin Prison. After his release, he sailed to Japan, and was never heard from again.

In the early years of this century, the young Dutch artist Hans Van Meegeren had enormous success. Buyers snatched up his paintings as fast as he could produce them. Then the critics turned against him, and people stopped buying his paintings. He was forced to design Christmas cards for a living.

This change in fortune left Van Meegeren very embittered. He determined to revenge himself on the critics. He would prove that they knew nothing about art.

It took him four years to make a perfect copy of a painting by Jan Vermeer, the great seventeenth-century Dutch master. He scraped the paint off an old canvas and put his painting in its place. He only used paints that were like those available to Vermeer. And he baked the finished painting in an oven to give it a true antique look.

Then Van Meegeren spread the rumor that a little-known Vermeer painting had just been smuggled out of Italy. Just as he planned, the story came to the attention of critic Dr. Bredius, one of Van Meegeren's enemies. After studying it carefully, Dr. Bredius proclaimed the forgery a "glorious work of Vermeer."

The painter was overjoyed that he had fooled Dr. Bredius. He was even more delighted to receive a large sum of money for the fake Vermeer. Instead of exposing the art expert, Van Meegeren started producing more forgeries.

During World War II, one of Van Meegeren's forged paintings was sold to a Nazi official. At the war's end, Van Meegeren was charged with the crime of dealing with the enemy. To defend himself, the painter told the court that the work—and all the other paintings he had sold—were fakes. But no one believed him!

Van Meegeren then offered to create an "original Vermeer" in front of police witnesses. The public was dazzled by Van Meegeren's skill, and sympathized with him. But the judge had to uphold the law. He sentenced the painter to one year in jail. The ailing Van Meegeren, however, died before his term started.

These are a few brief examples of bizarre crimes. The rest of this book contains more complete accounts of several famous—as well as strange or unusual—robberies, forgeries, and swindles. Some are bizarre because of the nature of the crime itself; others because of the huge sums of money involved. The brilliance of some of the criminals will astound you; the stupidity of others may appall you. However, all will fascinate you—especially since every story is absolutely true!

CHAPTER ONE

Martin Guerre: Amazing Imposter

Late one afternoon in 1557, in the village of Artigat in southern France, a slim young woman, Bertrande, was sitting in a corner of her garden. Her eight-year-old son, Sanxi, was playing at her feet. Two young women were standing and talking at the far end of the garden.

Bertrande was lost in thought. She was recalling, as she often did, something that had happened not long after the birth of her little boy. She had been quarreling with her husband. So angry had he made her, that she struck him a blow on the face. Without uttering a word, her husband turned and left. Bertrande had not seen or heard from him since. In fact, no one knew what had happened to Martin Guerre.

As Bertrande sighed deeply and reached out to touch the boy, she noticed a man approaching the garden gate. When he drew close, the newcomer was embraced by the girls. "It is our brother Martin," they shouted.

Bertrande's heart leapt. The man quickly strode to where Bertrande sat. She stood up, but she did not speak.

"My darling Bertrande," the stranger whispered. "Do you not know me . . . your own Martin?"

Still she did not reply. One of the girls came up to her. "Bertrande, speak! It is Martin, your husband, our brother. He's come back. Speak to him!"

Bertrande bowed her head. She could not believe that this man who gazed at her so fondly was really her long-lost husband. He looked so much like Martin Guerre, and yet he was different. Had she forgotten her husband's features after all these years? Before she could get her thoughts straight, the man clasped her to him and kissed her. She fainted in his arms.

In truth, the man was not Martin Guerre. He was an imposter—a pretender—playing the role of Bertrande's husband. The story of how this came about is one of the most bizarre in all history.

After Martin Guerre left his wife on that fateful day, he had joined the army. By a strange coincidence he had become close friends with another soldier, Arnauld de Tily, nicknamed Ponselle. The two were so much alike that they were often taken for twins. They were identical down to the shape of their teeth, the warts on their hands, and the scar each bore on his forehead. Martin totally trusted his comrade and told him the most personal and intimate details of his life.

During one battle, Martin was shot in the leg. Ponselle rushed to help the wounded man. Sure that he was going to die, Martin asked Ponselle to grant him one last request.

"Go to my wife," he said. "Tell her I died fighting for my country. She will be so pleased." Then Martin closed his eyes.

Believing that Martin had breathed his last, Ponselle stooped over the body. He went through his friend's pockets and removed all the money, identification, and personal papers he found there. Suddenly, he was struck by an exciting thought: Why not become Martin Guerre? All that belonged to Martin could now belong to him. With that, Ponselle slipped away from his army post in the dead of night. He set out for the village of Artigat to put his plan into action.

Within a few days, Ponselle had taken up the life of Martin Guerre. His wife and child had come to accept him as husband and father. The rest of the villagers, too, took him up warmly. They befriended him and listened avidly to tales of his adventures.

After establishing himself in the village, Ponselle went to see Martin's uncle, Pierre Guerre. He asked for an accounting of the property and money he had looked after while Martin was gone.

"Now that I am returned," Ponselle said, "I want to take charge of my own estate."

The uncle listened and then said, "The estate is gone. I sold everything to keep your wife and child while you were away."

Ponselle raised his hand as if to strike Pierre. "I vow never to forgive you for this," he cried.

"And I, too, will never forget!" replied Pierre in great anger.

In fact, Pierre suspected from the start that Ponselle was an imposter. Now he was awaiting proof.

The months flew by and Bertrande and her husband lived very happily together. They were a loving and caring couple. She also had another child now. Any doubts about Ponselle had long since vanished. She loved her husband more than ever. Little did she know that a terrible calamity was about to rob her of all joy and pleasure.

Not long after the baby's christening, two former soldiers wandered into Artigat. They met Ponselle in the village square and hailed him as their comrade, Ponselle. He reacted in anger. "My name is Martin Guerre!" he declared.

But the two strangers insisted. They knew the real Martin Guerre, and he had lost his leg in battle.

This was the moment Uncle Pierre Guerre had been waiting for. He signed a form for the arrest of the bogus Martin Guerre.

The judge came to the village to hear testimony from the villagers. Most everyone believed Ponselle when he claimed to be Martin Guerre. Even Martin's sisters and aunts said that he was no imposter. They insisted that Uncle Pierre had evil motives, since only he would gain if Ponselle was found guilty. Through it all, Bertrande stood by her husband.

"Declare for all the court to hear if I am an imposter," Ponselle cried out to Bertrande.

And Bertrande, looking very composed, said, "You are my husband. I know you. And I love you."

There was not enough evidence against Ponselle. The judge ordered him to be released. Ponselle resumed his life as Martin Guerre.

Accounts differ as to what happened next in this strange tale. However, most agree that news of the hearing reached the real Martin Guerre, who had not died during the battle where he had been wounded. Angry at his friend, and eager to see justice done, Martin returned to his village. He appeared in the town square dressed in torn, dusty clothes, limping on his wooden leg. Bertrande was called from the laundry. Ponselle came in from the fields. As soon as Bertrande saw the newcomer she knew the awful truth.

The villagers watched as the two men glared at each other. They wondered at the close resemblance. Every detail of their appearance was the same. The only difference was the newcomer's wooden leg.

The authorities were summoned, and a new trial was ordered. The atmosphere in the courtroom was tense. Every seat was taken, and people squeezed into every inch of the large room. Over thirty witnesses were called. About half said that Ponselle was the real Martin Guerre. The other half insisted that it was the other way around.

One person to give testimony was the village bootmaker. He held up two wooden shoe molds. They showed that the original Martin Guerre's foot was a larger size than the man now accused of being the imposter.

At the end of the long trial, Bertrande was brought face to face with the two men. A hush fell over the crowd. After a long pause, the judge spoke. "Woman, you must make the choice. Which one is your real husband?"

Bertrande slowly looked from man to man. One had deserted her, and had gone off without a thought for her or their child. The other had given her many years of love and affection. Tears streamed down her cheeks. The color drained from her face. It seemed an eternity before she moved. But then, slowly, she stepped forward. She dropped to her knees before the real Martin Guerre.

Bertrande's true husband took no notice of her. He stared straight ahead. But Ponselle, the imposter, reached out to her. With love in his eyes, he helped her to her feet.

Then came another shock for Bertrande. Looking scornfully at her, Martin Guerre declared in a very loud voice, "It is your fault that this happened. You took this man into your house even though you knew he was an imposter. You should be on trial. You are a liar and an adulterer!"

The trial came to an end. The prisoner was found guilty and sentenced to be hanged. Bertrande sobbed loudly as the judge read the verdict.

The entire town of Artigat turned out for the public hanging. As he was led to the gallows, Ponselle searched among the upturned faces for Bertrande. She was not to be seen. Right after the trial, she had fallen ill. And at the very moment Ponselle was being executed she lay dying—many say of a broken heart.

CHAPTER TWO

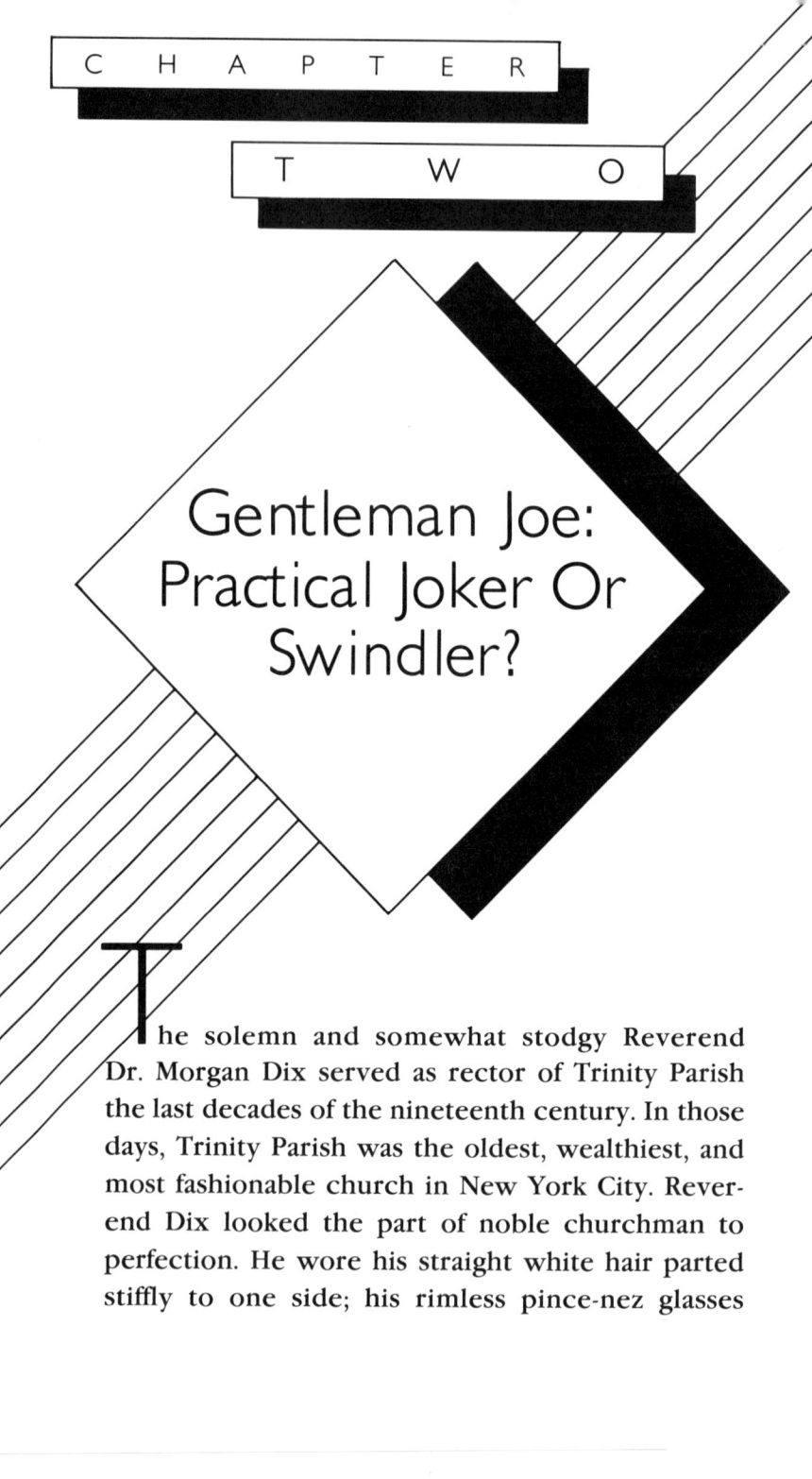

Gentleman Joe: Practical Joker Or Swindler?

The solemn and somewhat stodgy Reverend Dr. Morgan Dix served as rector of Trinity Parish the last decades of the nineteenth century. In those days, Trinity Parish was the oldest, wealthiest, and most fashionable church in New York City. Reverend Dix looked the part of noble churchman to perfection. He wore his straight white hair parted stiffly to one side; his rimless pince-nez glasses pinched the bridge of his narrow nose. From his high pulpit, clad in a flowing white gown, the upright minister was an imposing figure of the utmost seriousness.

On the morning of Wednesday, February 18, 1880, a letter arrived at the rectory addressed to Reverend Dix. It was from the Acme Safe Company. They thanked him for requesting information on their safes. Enclosed was a brochure and price list. It further stated that a salesman would soon call to take his order.

Looking more grim than usual, Reverend Dix carefully folded the letter and returned it to its envelope. He had not written to Acme, and he did not wish any salesman to call. In fact, the entire situation unnerved him. He would ask his secretary to send Acme a note pointing out the error.

Before the letter could be written, the doorbell rang. It was the Acme salesman. Reverend Dix explained the misunderstanding. The surprised salesman showed the reverend a postal card. Written as plain as could be, in the rector's own hand, was a request for information on safes.

The rectory bell rang again about ten minutes later. This time the caller was a teacher from St. John's School for Girls. According to Reverend Dix's instructions, he was there to enroll twenty girls from Trinity Parish at St. John's. The reverend was confused at first. Then his narrow lips tightened. He became very pale. The man at the door pulled out a postal card. On the card, over Reverend Dix's signature, was the enrollment request.

"That card is a forgery," Reverend Dix loudly protested. "Someone is playing a practical joke on me—and I'm *not* amused!"

As the reverend showed the gentleman out, he noticed someone else tying two giant bay horses to the hitching post in front of his house. When this person came to the door, he told a similar tale. The horse auctioneer had received a card from Reverend Dix asking that a matched set of carriage horses be delivered.

"And how did the reverend wish to pay for them?" the man politely asked.

While they were discussing the matter, merchants from another safe company, a lock manufacturer, and several stores that sold stoves and iceboxes appeared in turn at the door to the rectory. All graciously thanked the reverend for writing to them and offered to fill his order. A wig maker arrived with a number of samples for a fitting. The director of a large dancing school showed up to make arrangements to teach the waltz step to the staff of the Sunday school.

By the end of the day, Reverend Dix was very sorely vexed. Who had sent out so many bogus postal cards in his handwriting? And why, in heaven's name, had they done so?

If Reverend Dix thought that things would be better the next day, he was gravely mistaken. The steady stream of letters and callers picked up in volume. Now dealers in organs and pianos, farm equipment, breakfast food, shoe polish, patent medicines, fire extinguishers, Bibles, and plumbing supplies, among many others, dropped by the rectory.

Day after day a parade of merchants, peddlers, hawkers, and hucksters trooped up the steps and marched down again. A full twenty-eight dealers in used clothing popped up at fifteen-minute intervals on one snowy day. They all had cards saying that Reverend Dix was selling his wife's wardrobe. Some pawnbrokers thought the church's silver chest was for sale. Toward the end of the week, twenty doctors showed up over a twenty-four-hour period to treat Reverend Dix for assorted complaints.

After nine days, the flood of visitors came to an abrupt halt. The postman brought a single letter. For $1,000, the message related, the annoyances would stop forever. If the reverend agreed to pay the money, he should place the following personal ad in the *New York Herald*: "Gentleman Joe—all right. M.D."

Reverend Dix did not know what to do. This was more than a practical joke. It was extortion. Perhaps the authorities could do something. He contacted James Gayler of the post office and Captain Thomas Byrnes of the New York City police department. They agreed to investigate the case, and they advised him not to place the newspaper ad.

The very next day, there was another stampede. In the morning, a group of shoe salesmen presented themselves to Reverend Dix. Each was carrying a large box of sample shoes. At noon, fourteen clergymen came for lunch, all bearing their postal-card invitations. Later that day, a dozen or so angry husbands pounded on the reverend's door to denounce him for sending love notes to their wives.

Once more, a letter arrived from Gentleman

Joe. He asked again for the $1,000. This time he asked that it be paid through Daniel Buckley, owner of a Third Avenue bar. The law officers contacted Buckley. The poor man knew nothing of Gentleman Joe's caper. What's more, he was the victim of a practical joke. One day he noticed that his bar was much busier than usual. And all the patrons kept thanking him for his kindness. Later he learned that someone had placed an ad in the *Herald* saying that Mr. Buckley would be giving that day's receipts to the Irish Relief Fund!

Then, for almost a month, no one heard from Gentleman Joe. All cards and callers stopped coming. Reverend Dix was able to devote himself fully to his church work for the first time since the beginning of the disturbing incidents. However, on March 17, it all started again. A letter from Gentleman Joe said that the fee for relief had risen to $1,500. Unless the reverend placed a personal ad in the paper, the annoyances and cards would resume.

True to his word, on March 19, an army of household servants appeared at the rectory. All claimed that they had just been hired by Reverend Dix. An undertaker then came to claim a body. A tattoo artist appeared to decorate the reverend's chest. And four lawyers paid a professional visit to the reverend to advise him on obtaining a divorce.

By this time everyone knew about the woes that had befallen the poor Reverend Dix. The newspapers were making sensational stories of each day's events. Among those who read about the case was Samuel T. Peters, a broker on the cotton exchange. Mr. Peters had recently returned from a trip to New Orleans.

The incident reminded Peters of a similar case that had taken place seven years earlier. While in London on business, Peters had met Eugene Fairfax Williamson. He knew Williamson slightly as a former Sunday school teacher at Trinity Parish. Williamson asked Peters to testify on his behalf at a trial in which he was accused of annoying his landlord, Adolph Rosenbaum. According to Rosenbaum, Williamson had sent all sorts of salespeople to the Rosenbaum house. Guests arrived for fictitious dinner parties. Messengers hand-delivered steamship tickets to such faraway destinations as Hong Kong and Calcutta. Once, though, Rosenbaum saw Williamson watching through the window of a nearby house. He was laughing at Rosenbaum's difficulties in handling all the callers.

The jury found Williamson guilty. He was sentenced to one year in jail.

Peters lost little time in telling his story to Captain Byrnes of the police department. Byrnes asked Reverend Dix to try to recall Williamson from Trinity Parish. But the haughty man could not. Reverend D. Edward Noyes from St. Alban's Church, however, did remember Williamson. He described the one-time teacher as red-haired, bearded, short, and always well dressed. The suspect, he said, spoke well, had a British accent, and was both charming and witty. He seemed to have plenty of money because he traded in the finest shops, ate in the best restaurants, and roomed at the most expensive hotels. With this description, Byrnes and his men set out to find Williamson.

At the same time, James Gayler struck out in a different direction. A man named Williamson, he learned by questioning other clergymen, had been asked to leave Trinity Parish after some sort of trouble. This might be the motive for targeting Reverend Dix. Gayler was also studying the two Gentleman Joe letters. The paper, he noticed, was torn across the top. He had probably ripped off the letterhead that would help to identify him.

On a hunch, Gayler's group combed the city for matching hotel stationery. At the luxury Windsor Hotel on Fifth Avenue they found the identical paper.

Upon checking the hotel's register, Gayler found Williamson's signature. It was in the same well-rounded script that appeared on the postal cards. According to the hotel record, Williamson had checked in on February 14, just before the siege on Reverend Dix began. He had checked out nine days later, about the time the cards and callers had stopped. And on March 14 he returned, just before the second onslaught.

The hotel manager staunchly defended Mr. Williamson. He said he was a fine gentleman who always paid his bills on time and was a most generous tipper. Nevertheless, both Byrnes and Gayler believed that they had found their man. Just one problem remained: Williamson had checked out hours before. Only his big trunk was still in New York, awaiting shipment to Baltimore.

Gayler and his men went to Baltimore. They were able to trace Williamson, and arrested him without any trouble. In fact, the sophisticated and well-mannered Williamson seemed almost relieved to be caught. He confessed to everything.

Brought back to New York, Williamson was booked on charges of forgery and extortion. At the trial on April 26, 1880, several facts came to light. Williamson had indeed been dismissed from Trinity Parish after a scandal involving a choir boy. Reverend Dix, however, had not been involved in that case. Williamson had also once been found guilty of a similar charge with another young man. In that case, he had jumped bail and was therefore a fugitive from justice. Moreover, he had published four books that were word-for-word copies of others. Hence, the charge of plagiarism was added to the rest.

Based on his confession, the jury found Eugene Fairfax Williamson, alias Gentleman Joe, guilty as charged. The judge imposed a harsh sentence—three and one-half years at hard labor. After the trial, Williamson had told reporters, "I'll never live through it." His prophecy proved correct. He died on December 22, scarcely eight months after entering prison.

To the end, though, Gentleman Joe remained a puzzling figure. How had he supported himself in such high style with no apparent source of income? Why did he choose Reverend Dix as his target? And finally, was it all a foolish prank or a criminal attempt at extortion?

The answers, unfortunately, will never be known.

CHAPTER THREE

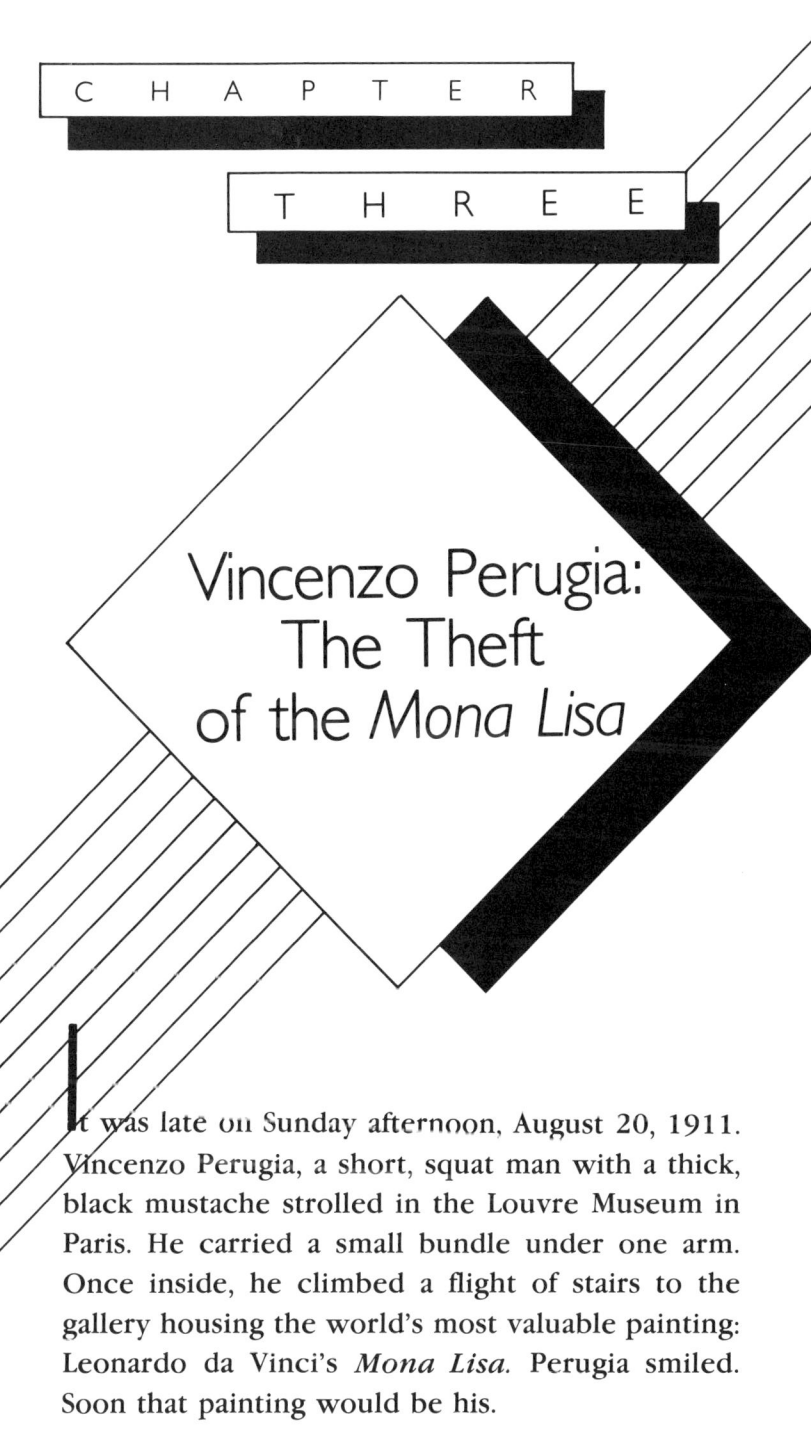

Vincenzo Perugia: The Theft of the *Mona Lisa*

It was late on Sunday afternoon, August 20, 1911. Vincenzo Perugia, a short, squat man with a thick, black mustache strolled in the Louvre Museum in Paris. He carried a small bundle under one arm. Once inside, he climbed a flight of stairs to the gallery housing the world's most valuable painting: Leonardo da Vinci's *Mona Lisa.* Perugia smiled. Soon that painting would be his.

At about the same time, the Lancelotti brothers, Vincent and Michele, entered the Louvre through different doors. They headed to the same gallery. Although they exchanged knowing glances with Perugia, no one spoke.

A bored museum guard glanced at his watch—just one hour until closing time. The next day the museum was not open to the public. Monday was reserved for cleaning the museum, and for changing and repairing the exhibits.

Just before four o'clock, the guard started asking people to leave. As everyone headed toward the exits, Perugia and the Lancelotti brothers ducked into an empty gallery. Checking to see that no one was looking, they opened a door set in a wall. They quickly stepped inside the small storeroom. This would be their hiding place until morning.

After a restless night in the cramped space, the men awoke at about seven o'clock. Perugia opened his package and removed three white tunics that looked like lab coats. They were identical to the uniforms worn by the workers at the Louvre on clean-up days.

Now Perugia and his two partners hurried out of their little room. They walked purposefully toward the *Mona Lisa*. In a moment, Perugia unscrewed the priceless art work from the wall. The painting, on a wooden panel inside a large carved frame covered by thick glass, was quite heavy. With Vincent's help, Perugia carried it down the hall, while Michele trailed behind. Not one of the busy workers even turned to look at the trio.

The intruders then carried the treasure through a door that led to a dark, narrow staircase. There Perugia deftly removed the precious panel from its frame and glass case. Tucking the painting under his arm, he fairly flew down the stairs, with the Lancelottis at his heels.

At the foot of the stairs there was a terrible surprise! The door was locked!

Perugia had a duplicate key, but it did not fit the lock. Now desperate, he sent Michele up the stairs to keep watch. Using the same screwdriver he had used before, he started to remove the entire lock. He was so busy that he almost missed Michele's warning, "For heaven's sake, stop. Someone's coming!"

The museum's plumber had started down the darkened stairs. Seeing the men at the door, he asked, "What's going on?"

"Some fool stole the doorknob," shouted Perugia. "How are we supposed to get out of here?"

Reaching into his tool kit, the plumber pulled out a pair of pliers. Pushing on the latch, he opened the door.

"I'll let someone know it's broken," said the workman as he walked away.

"Good idea," Perugia called back as they headed in the opposite direction toward a door that led to the street. There was only one problem. A guard mopping the floor blocked their way. Then luck was with them. The man left to change the water in his pail. Hugging the painting under his white coat, Perugia and his two cohorts strode out of the museum.

Paris was just waking up as the men exited and jumped into a waiting taxi. The cabbie took them across town, to the home of Vincent's girlfriend. According to their plan, they hid the painting in her tiny attic room. Perugia then dashed off to his regular job as a carpenter. His boss accepted the excuse that he was late because he had overslept.

That evening the three men met at the girlfriend's apartment. They were joined by Marqués Eduardo de Valfierno. Valfierno was the youngest son of a once wealthy family of Argentinian landowners. His only source of income now was the money he made selling off his family's art treasures. The theft of the *Mona Lisa* was part of Valfierno's wild scheme to make his fortune.

Valfierno had used a partner to carry out the first part of his plan. He was Yves Chaudron, an extraordinary artist who could turn out perfect copies of old paintings. Over the past months, Chaudron had made six duplicates of the *Mona Lisa*. He imitated every line, shape, color, and brush stroke of the original.

Valfierno had next enlisted the help of Perugia. Perugia had once worked at the Louvre. While there, he had installed the glass shield on the *Mona Lisa*. Perugia still knew his way around the huge museum. The Lancelotti brothers were called on to help Perugia.

Valfierno knew that the entire art world would soon hear about the robbery. Then he would be able to sell the six copies as originals. And each greedy buyer would think he alone was getting the stolen painting!

Now that the theft was over, Valfierno was very pleased. He paid the men the money he had promised, and told Perugia to await further instructions. More cash would be coming for him.

The theft was not discovered until the museum opened on Tuesday. A force of one hundred policemen rushed in to search the vast building. All they found was the empty frame and glass in the stairwell. By five-thirty that evening, banner headlines around the world carried the news of the robbery. The French compared it to stealing a tower of the Notre Dame Cathedral. A sizable reward was offered for the painting's return.

Once the theft was known, Valfierno took his next step. He sold the six copies of the *Mona Lisa* that Chaudron had prepared. Each customer was told that he was getting the stolen original. Details of the sales are not known. But it is believed that each paid around $300,000 for a forgery.

The police followed every possible lead. All cars, trains, and ships leaving France were checked. Everyone who had anything to do with the Louvre was questioned—but to no avail.

At one point the investigators nearly caught Perugia. They found a left thumbprint on the glass case left in the stairwell. Since Perugia had a police record, copies of his fingerprints were on file. However, the police had only taken prints of his right hand. They were not able, therefore, to identify him.

After he was cleared, Perugia moved the original painting to his room. He built a trunk with a false bottom. With the painting hidden there, he felt safer. The rest of the trunk was filled with old clothes. Now he awaited the final payment Valfierno had promised for his part in the robbery.

Valfierno, though, was no longer interested in Perugia or the original painting. And he thought that he had paid Perugia enough. So he went on an extended holiday to North Africa and the Middle East.

Back in Paris, Perugia waited and brooded. Expecting more money, he had squandered all the cash he had been given. Finally, after two years, he made up his mind. He would take matters into his own hands.

In November 1913, Italian-born Perugia hit on a scheme. He would return the *Mona Lisa* to Italy where it had been painted. It would bring him his rightful share of the money. And it would also punish the French for the way they treated him and other Italians living in Paris.

Perugia wrote to an art dealer in Florence. He agreed to pay Perugia $100,000 for the painting—if it was authentic.

On December 11, the art dealer met Perugia at the small hotel in Florence where Perugia was staying. The expert examined the painting and convinced himself that it was the original *Mona Lisa.* As soon as he left, though, the dealer called the police. Perugia was arrested.

Perugia went on trial on June 4, 1914, in Florence. Many believed him when he claimed to have stolen the painting for patriotic reasons. He wanted to restore it to its rightful home, he said.

The judges first sentenced Perugia to a year in

jail. But after hearing pleas for mercy, they reduced the sentence to seven months. By then, Perugia had already served more than seven months. He was set free.

It was nearly three years since Perugia had walked out of the Louvre with the *Mona Lisa* under his arm. The painting was now safely back at the Louvre. Perugia was a free man living in his native Italy. No one knows for certain what became of the six Chaudron copies. And surely no one ever dreamed of Valfierno's role in the plot.

If all this sounds too bizarre to be true, go to Via Panzani in Florence. Find the Hotel La Gioconda (another name for the *Mona Lisa*). There you will read the following: "In this hotel, in 1913, was recovered *La Gioconda,* stolen from the Louvre."

CHAPTER FOUR

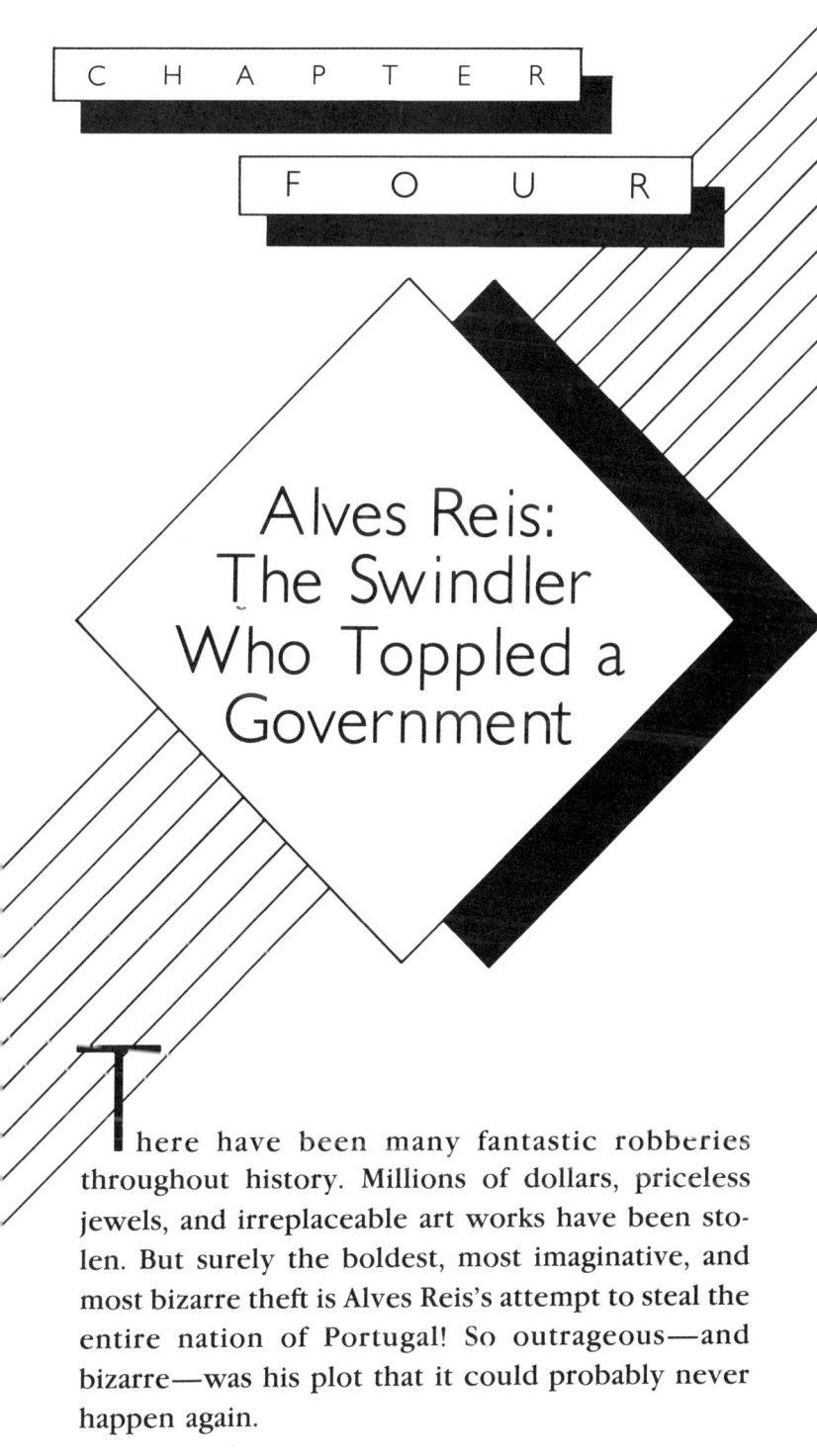

Alves Reis: The Swindler Who Toppled a Government

There have been many fantastic robberies throughout history. Millions of dollars, priceless jewels, and irreplaceable art works have been stolen. But surely the boldest, most imaginative, and most bizarre theft is Alves Reis's attempt to steal the entire nation of Portugal! So outrageous—and bizarre—was his plot that it could probably never happen again.

Counterfeiting—printing fake money—was at the heart of Reis's scheme. But he knew that almost all counterfeit scams fail. The fake money is always recognized. It is impossible to duplicate exactly the printing plates, the paper, and the inks of the original money. It is also very hard to put the money into circulation without getting caught. And to make it worse, those who are convicted of counterfeiting are punished severely, since it is a crime against the state. So Reis made a plan that he considered foolproof.

Reis's idea was to forge papers showing that he and a group of financiers were lending the economically troubled Portuguese colony of Angola 100 million escudos ($5 million). In return, Reis had the right to have 100 million escudo bank notes printed by Portugal's official printer, using official government plates, paper, and ink.

Alves Reis hatched his brainstorm on November 24, 1924, when he was twenty-eight years old. Over the following months, Reis assembled an international "gang" of businessmen and financiers: Jóse Bandeira (Portugal), Karl Marang (Holland), and Adolf Hennies (Germany). All were wealthy and successful, yet each had made some shady business deals.

In Portugal, as in all other countries, only the government has the authority to issue money. Reis's first move, therefore, was to forge a letter, presumably from the official bank, the Bank of Portugal. In return for the loan, the letter said, Reis had permission to have 100 million escudos printed.

Reis sent Karl Marang to London with the forged document. He went to Waterlow and Sons, London—the regular printer of Portugal's paper money. Waterlow held the original printing plates and the proper paper and inks to turn out Portuguese bank notes.

Marang spoke to Sir William Waterlow, the distinguished director of the firm. He explained why the whole transaction had to be kept secret. If news leaked out that Portugal was printing $5 million worth of escudos, he told Waterlow, the value of the currency would go down, causing severe economic problems.

Sir William went along with Marang's wish to keep the matter quiet. Still, he wanted to ask the director of the Bank of Portugal for permission to use the official 500-escudo plates to print this new money. Marang cleverly offered to deliver the request letter in person. Sir William agreed. Of course, Marang promptly turned the letter over to Reis.

Reis lost no time in forging a new letter, which Marang now brought back to Sir William. Not long after, Waterlow started production. Marang picked up the first shipment: 20,000 500-escudo notes, worth about a half-million dollars. They were identical in every way to authentic 500-escudo notes.

Having the counterfeit bills in hand raised new problems for Reis. Even exact duplicates of legitimate bills needed to be spent wisely to avoid suspicion. By recruiting some shady currency dealers to buy foreign money, Reis obtained dollars, pounds, francs, and marks for the escudo bills. The foreign currency was deposited in special bank accounts.

Reis also opened about a dozen regular bank accounts with the new money. When he later withdrew the money, though, he was always given different bills. Opening these accounts did more than get the bogus bills into circulation. They also proved to Reis that his money was accepted by everyone.

After Reis received the last shipment of escudo notes, he opened his own bank: Bank of Angola & Metropole. Through this front, Reis funneled the money into extensive investments in Portugal and Angola. The bank, for example, owned 1.25 million acres of land in Angola alone.

The millions of dollars of counterfeit escudos quickly grew. Reis and his partners became multimillionaires. They purchased expensive homes and lavish estates, both in Lisbon and in the Portuguese countryside. The furnishings and the art works were the best that money could buy. Servants attended their every need. And they traveled about in the costliest limousines that were available.

Yet, their greed persisted. Reis now aimed to gain complete financial control over Portugal. To do this, he knew, he would have to take over the Bank of Portugal. He would then be the richest and most powerful man in the country, if not the world. However, he had another motive for this quest for power. Should his counterfeiting scheme be discovered, he might be able to protect himself from prosecution.

Reis's plan was to buy up shares in the bank until he held the controlling interest. By September, 1925, he and his partners had quietly acquired 7,000 of the 97,000 shares of the Bank of Portugal available to private investors. Slowly and secretly they were reaching their goal.

The small group of swindlers was really on top of the world now. They mixed with the most fashionable and respected citizens of the country. As highly privileged members of society, they were showered with praise and honors.

The first hint of trouble appeared in a Lisbon newspaper, *O Seculo,* on November 23, 1925. An article about the Bank of Angola & Metropole asked: Why is the bank buying up land and businesses in Portugal and Angola? Why are Reis and the others buying shares in the Bank of Portugal? And most embarrassing of all: Where is all the money coming from? The article hinted that a plot was underway, and called for an investigation.

Little more than a week later, on December 4, 1925, a clerk in a foreign currency dealer's office had an idea. He knew that Reis's bank had a standing offer to buy foreign currency from his firm above the official rate. One way to explain this strange behavior, he suggested, was that Reis was using counterfeit money.

A government official read the clerk's report. He ordered the seizure of all 500-escudo bills in the vault of one branch of the Bank of Angola & Metropole. A currency expert was called in to examine them. Much to everyone's surprise, he swore they were authentic.

Another expert was called in. He agreed that the bills were regular Portuguese 500-escudo bills. But as he went through the piles of bills, he found some duplicate serial numbers. On true currency they should all be different. The inevitable conclusion? The bills were counterfeit.

The officers of the Bank of Portugal met in an emergency session. The financial structure of the entire country was in danger. They had to do something about this massive counterfeiting scam. They voted immediately to recall *all* 500-escudo bills in circulation, and replace them with bills of other denominations.

Reis and Hennies were on their way back from a business trip to Angola when they got word that warrants were out for their arrest. Reis decided to turn himself in to the police. Hennies boarded a ship bound for Germany.

From his jail cell, Reis prepared more forged documents. One showed that the officers of the Bank of Portugal had taken part in the swindle. Another showed a receipt for a $25,000 bribe to the attorney general who was investigating the case. Accusations flew as everyone tried to protect himself by blaming someone else.

The government, weakened and paralyzed by the Reis affair, was overthrown by General Oscar Carmona in May 1926. He appointed Antonio Salazar as finance minister of the new regime. A powerful personality and effective politician, Salazar soon got control over the entire government. By 1932 he was a virtual dictator.

Alves Reis, considered the greatest swindler of all time, was tried and convicted. After serving eight years in prison and twelve years in exile, Reis went into business again.

It took far longer, however, for Portugal to restore a legitimate government. The rule of Salazar became one of the longest-lasting dictatorships in our time. And some say the troubles in Angola have not yet been entirely settled.

CHAPTER FIVE

Santa Claus: Wanted for Robbery

Two days before Christmas in 1927, a shiny new Buick automobile drove into the small town of Cisco, Texas. At the wheel was Robert Hill, barely twenty years old. Next to him sat Marshall Ratliff, twenty-four. In the back seat were Louis Davis, twenty-eight years old, and Henry Helms, thirty-two. Of the four, Davis was the only one who had never been in trouble with the law. Soon they would all be in more trouble than they ever dreamed possible.

The streets of Cisco were crowded that noon with last-minute shoppers. Store owners were saying that this Christmas season was the best ever. The farmers had brought in a good crop, and were in a mood for spending. So were the workers who had earned a lot of money in the oil fields to the east of town.

Most of the customers were on Avenue D, the main street of Cisco. Here, also, was the office of the First National Bank. And that's where the young men were heading.

A great deal of money had been deposited in the bank that day. The manager was a little worried. Small town banks, he knew, were popular targets for bank robbers. Thugs could break in easily, stage a holdup, and be out of town in a matter of minutes. A group of Cisco bankers was offering $5,000 to anyone who killed a bank robber caught in the act. The reward was supposed to stop future robberies. Some were afraid, though, that it would just make robberies more violent.

The blue Buick stopped at the railroad yard near the edge of town. Ratliff got out of the car. He wore a red flannel suit and stocking cap trimmed with soft white cotton. Most of his face was hidden behind a bushy white beard and heavy eyebrows. On his feet were a pair of shiny black boots.

"It's Santa Claus," a young boy said and pointed the figure out to his friend.

Many stopped to watch as Santa Claus strode

down Avenue D. As he headed toward the center of town, a crowd of youngsters and a few adults fell in behind him.

"What'll you bring me for Christmas?" one youngster said, tugging at Santa's baggy pants.

"You just be good," Santa answered. "You'll get some stuff."

"Where are you going, Santa?" a teenaged girl asked.

"You'll see. You'll see," he replied with a smile.

By the time Santa reached the one-story brick bank office, he had a crowd following him. And he was no longer smiling. Suddenly, he charged through the doors. Having parked in the alley next to the bank, his three accomplices rushed in with him. They drew guns.

"Stick 'em up," Hill snarled at a teller seated behind the marble counter.

Thinking it was a holiday prank, the teller, Jewell Poe, started to laugh. But the gunman yelled, "Move it! I mean business!"

Poe's arms shot up. So did the arms of the three other employees and the four customers in the bank at that moment.

That was the situation when six-year-old Frances Blasengame dragged her mother into the bank to talk to Santa Claus. Seeing the holdup in progress, Mrs. Blasengame wheeled around, pushing her daughter out ahead of her. Davis waved his gun at them, but he didn't shoot. They safely fled the bank.

"They're robbing the bank! First National!" Mrs. Blasengame screamed as she burst into the nearby police station.

Chief Bit Bedford jumped up. With shotgun in hand he ran at full speed toward the bank. In minutes, word of the robbery spread. From all sides people were running toward the bank. Many had guns. Quite a few were thinking of the $5,000 reward.

Meanwhile, Santa was behind the teller's counter. He forced Poe into the vault. Santa pulled a burlap sack marked "Idaho Potatoes" from under his shirt. The sack had served as padding for his costume.

"Fill it," he barked at Poe.

Grabbing handfuls of money, checks, stocks, and bonds, the unnerved bank teller hurried to load the sack. He shoved the money in as fast as he could. Then Santa pulled the bag shut.

"That's enough!" he roared, then said to his chums, "Let's beat it!"

The four thieves headed toward the door that led to the alley where they had parked the car. As they were leaving, though, they glanced at the front window. Someone was peering in—with a gun in his hand. One of the robbers—no one knows who—fired a shot through the window. Seconds later another shot rang out—this time from outside. Then the bandits started firing wildly at everyone they could see through the bank's windows. And from the outside came a hail of bullets.

The only hope of escape, Santa figured, was to take some hostages. So while Davis covered the front of the bank, Santa and the others herded eight hostages toward the door.

"Everyone in the car," yelled Helms. "And hurry."

Of course, everyone couldn't possibly fit into the sedan. Most managed to slip away in the confusion. Only two young girls, Laverne Comer, age twelve, and Emma May Robinson, age ten, who had come to the bank to withdraw money for Christmas shopping, got pushed into the car. Laverne was between Hill and Helms in the front seat; Emma was in the back.

As the Buick started to pick up speed, someone fired and blew out a rear tire. Hill almost lost control of the car, but somehow he made the turn onto Avenue D. Despite the flapping, smoking tire, the car lurched down the street, the crowd in hot pursuit.

By now Santa had smashed out the back window and was firing at the pursuers. Helms was throwing out fistfuls of huge nails to puncture the tires of the cars that had joined the chase.

The Buick gradually pulled a good distance ahead of the mob. The big problem now was the damage within. Davis had passed out from a bullet wound. Blood was gushing from Santa's chin. And Hill was straining to drive with only three good tires. That was when he noticed that they were almost out of gasoline. No one had thought to fill the tank!

At Fourteenth Street and Avenue D, the thieves saw a family driving into town in a brand-new Oldsmobile. Santa waved for them to stop and then ordered them all out of the car. They reluctantly obeyed. The robbers loaded the badly wounded Davis, the money sack, and the girls into the new car. Only then did they discover that the driver had run off with the key.

All this time, the posse was drawing closer. Unable to drive the Oldsmobile, the desperate men darted back to the Buick. They left the nearly dead Davis behind.

Even though the gas gauge indicated that the tank was empty, they were able to pull away. After a short stretch, they turned onto a narrow dirt road. It was then that one of them remembered the money. They had left the entire haul—about $12,000 in cash and $150,000 in checks and stocks—in the Oldsmobile!

The car got stuck in the brush less than a mile

down the road. The three men had no choice but to head into the woods. Santa told the girls to lie face down on the floor of the car and stay there. However, just before the men ran off, Laverne sneaked a look at Santa. She recognized him as Marshall Ratliff. Marshall was well known in Cisco. In fact, that's why he wore the Santa suit disguise that had caused him so much trouble.

The posse arrived a few minutes later. Guns drawn, they combed the countryside, but they couldn't find the men.

For nearly a week, the threesome eluded capture. Daringly, they walked back to Cisco to steal another car. They even had the nerve to drive to the house of Davis's sister. But the day the fugitives tried to run a sheriff's roadblock in the stolen car, their luck ran out. Marshall Ratliff was captured there and then. And the law caught up with Helms and Hill the very next day.

In the trials that began on January 16, the jury had no trouble reaching their verdicts. Marshall Ratliff and Henry Helms were found guilty of murder and sentenced to die in the electric chair. Robert Hill, who confessed to the robbery but claimed no part in the shooting, was given ninety-nine years.

Most people around Cisco, though, were not too happy with the outcome, especially Marshall's sentence. They didn't really believe that he would get the electric chair. He was getting off too easy, they said. They were also worried about a Texas law that said that a person who became insane in prison could not be executed until he became sane again.

Ratliff knew of this law. The jailers were not too surprised, therefore, when he began to show signs of mental illness, such as not eating and making jerky motions with his head and hands. They thought nothing of it when his speech became garbled and he quoted endlessly from the Bible. Even when he became like a vegetable—not moving or talking at all—they believed he was just trying to act insane.

All day and all night they spied on him, but he always behaved in the same strange way. Startling him, poking him, even burning him resulted in no response. His eyes remained blank. He even ignored his mother when she came to visit. At last even the most skeptical guard was convinced that Ratliff had indeed lost his mind.

From the middle of October until November 18, 1928, Ratliff lay like a corpse on his bunk. On that day, however, he caught his guards by surprise. When their backs were turned, he suddenly attacked them with a .38-caliber revolver.

"Give me the keys," he demanded.

A scuffle followed. Ratliff shot one guard and broke another's leg in the melee. Somehow one of the jailers managed to grab the gun. He used the handle to beat Ratliff unconscious.

Word of Ratliff's attack on the guard leaked out. Gradually, a crowd gathered outside the jail. By eight o'clock that evening, about one thousand angry people had come together.

"We want Santa Claus. We want Santa Claus," they chanted.

The cry grew louder and more angry.

Pack Kilborn, the sole guard on duty, spoke to the mob. "Ratliff's appeals have been denied. He's going to die in sixty days."

A few men stepped forward. "We're not going to wait. We've come to get Ratliff. Either you give him to us, or we take him."

Before Kilborn could say another word, several men grabbed him tightly. Rough hands tore at his keys. Then the mob leaders broke loose. They raced toward Ratliff's cell. About a dozen of them yanked the frantic prisoner off his bed. Holding him by his ankles, they dragged him down the iron staircase and out to the street. Once outside, they tied him up, slipped a noose around his neck, and hanged him from a tree.

The rope snapped and Ratliff struggled to his feet. A heavier rope was brought to the scene. This one held. Marshall Ratliff, alias Santa Claus, was dead.

At first the mob was exultant. "Santa Claus is dead! Santa Claus is dead!" they shouted. Then they grew quiet and began to disperse.

Sometime later, Helms was electrocuted in the electric chair. With Davis dead from his wounds and Hill in jail, the case of the Santa Claus robbery was closed. But the grisly death toll was not soon forgotten in the small town of Cisco. A total of nine policemen and townspeople, including Chief of Police Bit Bedford, was killed during that bloody day.

CHAPTER SIX

Tony Pino: The 1950 Brink's Holdup

The Brink's robbery in Boston on January 17, 1950 is world famous. The crime netted the gunmen about $2.8 million. It took six years to plan, but only twenty minutes to carry out. The investigation that followed also lasted six years. However, in the end, it was an informer's tip that helped solve the crime.

For roly-poly, Sicilian-born Anthony "Tony" Pino, the Brink's holdup was the climax of a lifetime of crime. His first arrest was at the age of eight, when he was picked up for riding a trolley without paying the fare. Convictions for a string of burglaries and robberies followed. Police and underworld figures came to know him as an ace safe-cracker. By the time he was released from jail on September 12, 1944, Pino had spent more than one-fourth of his thirty-seven years behind bars.

As part of his parole arrangement in 1944, Pino got a job working nights in a warehouse. Pino's shift ended at five in the morning, but the first train did not run until six. He usually spent the hour just walking around. It was on such a walk that he came across the place where Brink's armored vans, "money trucks" he called them, were kept. Each day the vans brought in the cash collected from Boston's stores and businesses. They also picked up equally large sums to be delivered to factories and businesses as payrolls.

The sight of money always made Tony eager to get his hands on it. His first thought was to hijack a Brink's truck as it made its rounds. To learn the routes and the amounts they carried, he trailed them throughout Boston. He also broke into an office across the street from the Brink's headquarters. From this hiding place, he watched the guards loading and unloading the trucks. However, he decided that the security arrangements were just too tight to bring off a successful hijacking.

The second idea Pino had was to burglarize the factories and offices where Brink's dropped off the payroll money. Several firms kept the money in an office safe overnight before giving out the pay envelopes. This plan worked. Pino frequently cracked open safes that were filled with extra cash. He was doing very well with these burglaries, but he wanted to do even better.

One day he slipped into the parking garage for the armored trucks. In an open cabinet he found all the trucks' keys. Pino grabbed a handful, made copies, and returned them before they were missed. Over the next weeks, Pino followed the different trucks. As soon as the guards went inside, Pino would open the back door with the key, snatch a money bag, and speed away. An estimated twenty such jobs netted him nearly $400,000. But that was still not enough.

By now Pino had a small gang. They knew the Brink's operation inside and out. And they felt ready to try a hijacking. Their target was truck forty-eight. Every week it delivered about $2 million for the payroll to the huge General Electric plant.

With three others, Pino lay in wait for truck forty-eight, but it never came. Something was wrong. At first they thought that they had been spotted. The actual explanation was much simpler. Brink's had moved to a new location: the North Terminal Garage building.

Pino switched his attention to the North Terminal Garage. Night after night he studied it very carefully. By watching, looking, touching, and listening to everything, he got to know the building very well. What he learned surprised him. The outside fire doors had no locks. There were no alarms on any of the inside doors. And there were no watchmen, or "hacks," on duty during the night.

Pino frequently sneaked into the garage after dark. He picked the locks of the Brink's offices. Inside the rooms, he made out the object of his search: an eight-foot-tall, eight-foot-wide, twelve-foot-long vault. The sight of the vault almost made Pino cry with joy. He could imagine the money it held. Before leaving, he kissed the safe.

Pino had to crawl around the unlit, gloomy garage now to find the alarm system on the vault, but he could find no wires. A sticker showed that the safe was protected by the ADT Security Service. Pino and a friend broke into the ADT office and stole the Brink's file. With this, the puzzle was solved. There were no wires because the vault was controlled by a *wireless* electronic alarm system.

Knowing that he could not disconnect the electronic alarm, Pino decided that they would go "heavy." They would force their way into the office some time when the vault was open.

Pino couldn't resist taking his gang members on tours of the Brink's offices. He showed them a clipboard with each day's schedule. It told the amount each truck would be carrying and how much would be in the vault at any one time. The smallest amount was about $3 million; the most was over $6 million.

Now he needed a plan to break into the vault room during working hours. The would-be robbers used powerful binoculars to spy into the room from a nearby roof. Countless hours were spent this way. They made their decision based on what they saw. Thursday seemed the best day for the heist; six o'clock in the evening was the best time, when the most money was in the vault. Also, the vault was not locked at that hour, and no more than five men were at work.

It was now the end of 1949, six years after Pino first got the idea for the heist. Pino had broken into the Brink's headquarters about seventy-five times. He had put together a gang of eleven men. At 6:10 P.M. on January 17, 1950, he sent out the word: The heist was on.

A truck and car picked up the men. Seven of them, wearing full-faced rubber Halloween masks, pea coats, and rubbers tiptoed up to the second-floor vault room. Poking their guns through the metal grille, one said, "Okay, boys, put them in the air."

Acting very quickly, some of the thieves used rope and tape to bind and gag the five employees. Others ransacked the vault. Pulling out empty sacks from under their coats, they stuffed them full of currency. After twenty frantic minutes, the crew's leader raised his hand and pointed to the door. Carrying, pushing, and dragging the heavy sacks, the crooks made their way out of the vault room and down the stairs.

Outside, Pino and the three others were shivering as they waited for the gunmen to emerge. Then they helped fling the bags into the back of the truck. With a squeal of the tires, the truck sped away. The entire operation took less than an hour, start to finish.

One employee broke free at 7:27 and called the police. By 7:45 police officers from the Boston police department filled the Brink's offices. A few minutes later, every bridge leading out of Boston was sealed off. Massachusetts state troopers checked passengers on every plane leaving the city. FBI agents arrived by ten o'clock. They took over the investigation of what was called "The Crime of the Century."

The FBI, along with the state and city police, launched one of the biggest manhunts in history. However, they were unable to develop any leads on the criminals, nor were they able to find or trace the masks, rubbers, or money bags the robbers had used. None of the guns were recovered. The authorities could not even pick up the trail the crooks followed after they left Brink's. And the evidence that did turn up—strands of rope, pieces of tape, and a chauffeur's cap—offered no clues to help identify the robbers.

Every Brink's employee and customer, past and present, was checked. All the sewers, warehouses, and graveyards in the area were searched for the loot. No leads at all were found.

The six employees who were held by the gunman—five guards and one garageman—were questioned at great length. The police strongly suspected that the heist was an inside job. But despite the intense grilling, they were unable to connect anyone with the crime. The pressure on the suspects, though, was so intense that five of them later suffered nervous breakdowns.

The FBI and the Boston police also applied pressure on all the known criminals in the city. Many were kept under 24-hour surveillance. Several were spot-checked at odd hours of the day and night. Dozens were picked up for questioning. Ten members of the actual Brink's gang, including Pino, were among them, but all were let go for lack of evidence.

Meanwhile, though, the weeks, months, and years were passing. The investigation had made no progress. They were not getting any closer to catching the criminals. Soon it was 1955, five years after the date of the heist. According to Massachusetts state law, a criminal not charged with a crime within six years is free, and can never be charged with that crime. The pressure was now on the police to catch the members of the gang. But it was proving harder and harder to turn up new evidence. They had little hope of success.

Then, late in 1955, "Specs" O'Keefe, one of the gang, got in touch with Pino. O'Keefe felt he had been cheated in his share of the loot and wanted more money. Pino refused. O'Keefe asked again. And once more Pino said no.

Finally, on January 6, 1956—exactly eleven days before the gang would have been safe forever—O'Keefe decided to take revenge on Pino. He confessed his role in the heist, and gave the names of the others. Working very quickly, the police rounded up the gang members. They beat the six-year deadline by a matter of days!

The trial began on August 6, 1956. All the thieves were found guilty and were sentenced to life imprisonment. Tony Pino, the genius behind the Brink's caper, served fourteen years and nine months before he was released on parole. On October 4, 1973, he died of a heart attack. His one regret was that he never got back at Specs O'Keefe for "ratting" on him.

CHAPTER SEVEN

Ronald Biggs: The Great Train Robbery

At first glance, it looked like a big, old, ordinary, red moving van. A closer look, though, showed that the roof of the truck was open. Inside was a collapsible tower—the kind that workers use to repair street lights and telephone wires.

No one gave the truck a second look as it slowly pulled up alongside the high wall of England's grim Wandsworth Prison at exactly 3:05 P.M. on July 8, 1965. It didn't even attract attention when the tower inside the truck started unfolding, carrying two men to the top of the prison wall. One carried a shotgun; the other threw down a rope ladder.

A prisoner in the exercise yard far below was waiting. He scurried up the ladder. Two guards started to give chase, but some other convicts got in their way, knocking them to the ground. Before they could get up, the prisoner was safely over the wall.

The escaped convict scampered into a small car just behind the van. Within moments both the van and car disappeared in the maze of London's side streets. Ronald Biggs, sentenced to thirty years in prison for his part in the 1963 Great Train Robbery, had successfully escaped. The role he played in the heist, and the life he had led after escaping from prison, make Biggs one of the most colorful figures in the history of crime.

Ronald Biggs, once a small-time crook, was brought into the raid on the Glasgow–London mail train quite accidentally. Two professional London thieves, Buster Edwards and Gordon Goody, were planning the job. They had heard that the first mail train after the August bank holiday weekend, would be carrying up to £5 million ($14 million at the exchange rate of the time) of unmarked bills in the second car behind the engine. They assembled a gang of fifteen men, including Roger Cordrey, an expert in train robberies. These skillful thieves let Biggs join them for one reason only: He knew a retired railroad engineer who would be able to drive the train for them.

The plan was to change two signal lights to stop

the train about thirty miles north of London. Then they would uncouple the engine and first two cars of the train and drive them forward about a mile down the track. The heavy sacks of bank notes would be loaded into a waiting truck and driven to their farmhouse hideaway. There they would count and divide the loot, and each man would go his own way.

Everything went according to plan, starting at about three o'clock on the morning of August 7. Robert Cordrey fixed the signals in the simplest way possible. He placed a heavy glove over the green lights in two signals. By hooking up batteries, he turned on the amber light in the first signal and the red light in the second one.

When the engineer saw the signal lights he brought the train to a halt. The gang members clambered aboard and seized the two men in the cab. They quickly uncoupled the engine and first cars. As it turned out, the engineer who Biggs had provided was not able to operate this engine. So the thieves had to force the train's engineer to drive the first part of the train down the tracks to where the truck was waiting.

The crooks allowed themselves one hour to break into the locked mail car, subdue the five clerks, load the bags into the truck, and drive to the secluded farm, about twenty miles away.

It didn't take them very long to count the money. The total came to over £2.5 million (almost $7.5 million). After all the expenses were paid, each gang member was given a share of about £150,000 ($420,000).

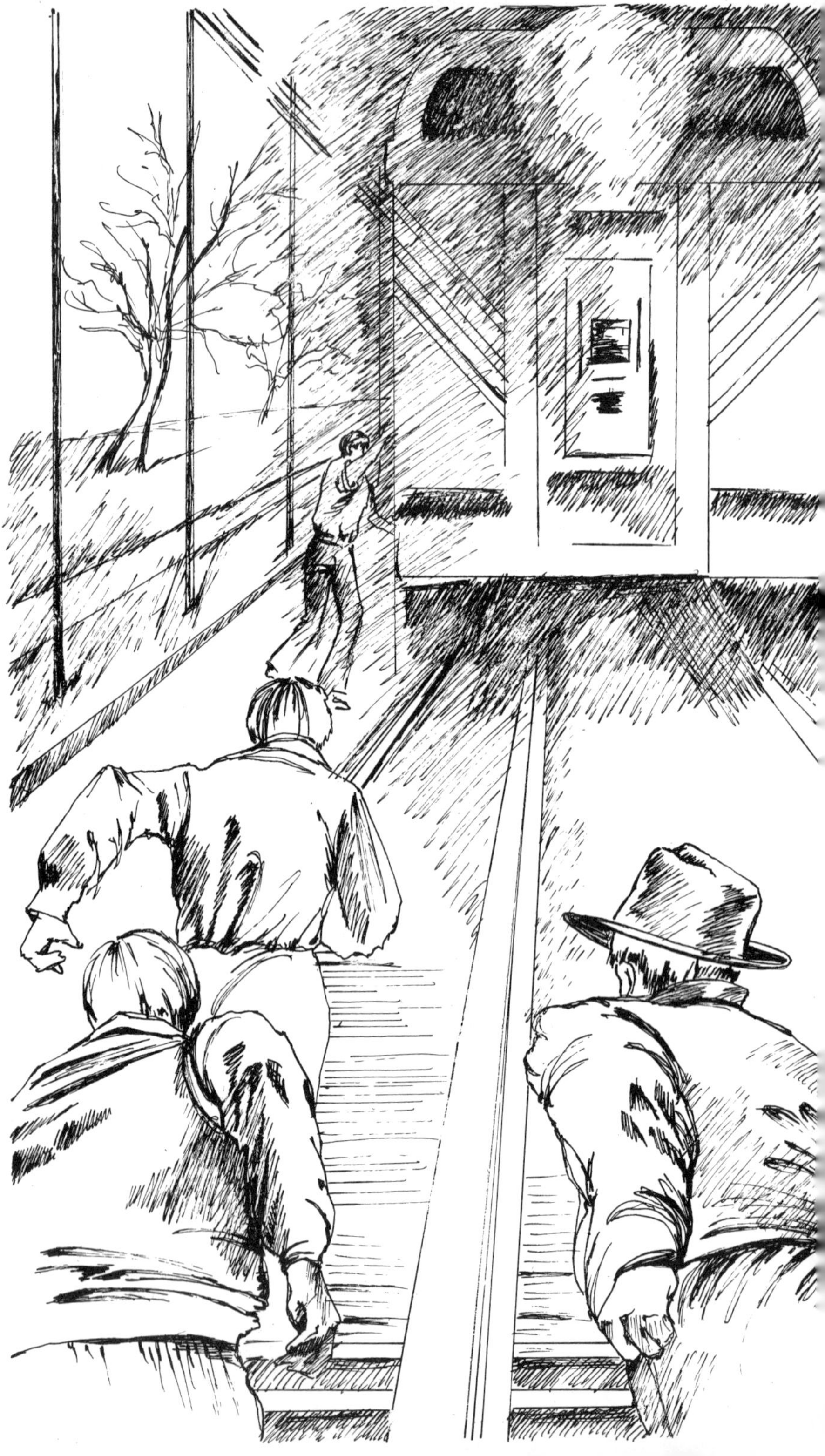

Scotland Yard and the local police got on the case at once, but they could find no clues. The criminals had covered their tracks very well. The farmhouse, where the thieves hid for a few days, was not discovered for a long time. One day, though, a passer-by noticed that the windows of the building were sealed with heavy black material. He called the police. The empty mailbags and other clues found there established the farmhouse as the train robbers' hideout.

Roger Cordrey was the first to be caught. He was picked up while he and a friend were trying to rent a private garage in which to keep the car that held Cordrey's share of the money. The garage owner, a policeman's widow, became suspicious when Roger's friend offered to pay three months rent in advance from a large roll of bills. She summoned the authorities. When Roger couldn't explain where he got so much cash, the police decided to search his car. There they found £56,000 ($156,800). The police realized that they had broken the case.

Over the following weeks, through good detective work, several tips, and a number of lucky breaks, most of the other men were arrested. The trial began on January 20, 1964, and lasted a little more than two months. All were found guilty; most received sentences of thirty years.

However, the story does not end there. One of those who evaded capture was finally arrested in 1968. Another who safely fled to Mexico was so homesick that he returned to England, where he gave himself up, and received a fifteen-year term.

Still another went to prison, escaped, and lived in Canada until he was picked up there in 1981.

And on that July afternoon in 1965, Ronald Biggs scaled the wall of Wandsworth Prison and found himself a free man. From London he made his way to Australia where, instead of returning to a life of crime, he tried to earn a legitimate living. At first he managed a run-down hotel; then he went back to his old trade as a carpenter. Unfortunately, in 1969 a story about the Great Train Robbery appeared in an Australian magazine. Biggs was recognized by his photograph. One jump ahead of the police, he managed to get aboard a ship bound for Brazil.

Biggs led the good life in South America. He worked as handyman for a Swiss stockbroker. Always handsome and charming, he surrounded himself with beautiful women, jazz, good books, and gourmet food. However, his pleasant lifestyle was shattered on the afternoon of Friday, February 1, 1974, when Chief Superintendent Slipper of Scotland Yard suddenly appeared in Biggs's room.

"Nice to see you again, Ronnie," said Slipper. "It's been a long time."

The Brazilian police, who had accompanied Slipper, clapped Biggs in jail until the papers for his return to England could be prepared.

Biggs's extraordinary good luck, however, stayed with him. His Indian girlfriend, Raimunda, declared that she was pregnant with his child. Since Brazilian law forbids deportation of the father of a Brazilian child, Biggs was allowed to remain in the country.

In 1981 Ronald Biggs had another close call. Some British adventurers tried to kidnap him. They wanted to bring him back to England for the huge sums they would earn for book and film rights to their story. The yacht that they were using, however, was seized by the navy of the island of Barbados. Biggs was allowed to return to Brazil. Even the British seemed relieved that the kidnapping attempt had failed. Few wanted Biggs to be returned to England in this degrading manner.

The last time Biggs received world attention was at the end of 1982. Bronzed and suave-looking, Biggs appeared in a television commercial. He was shown on the terrace of his apartment overlooking the Copacabana Beach in Rio de Janeiro. With a coy smile, Biggs held up a can of Café de Rio coffee, looked into the camera, and said: "Living here in Rio, I have lots of coffees to choose from. When you're *on the run* like me, you appreciate a good cup of coffee."

CHAPTER EIGHT

Charlie Marzano: The Purolator Heist

*B*eep—*Beep*—*Beep*—*Beep.*

The ear-splitting blasts from the horn filled the alarm room of the Wells Fargo Security office in Chicago.

Beep—*Beep*—*Beep*—*Beep.*

The painfully loud sounds kept coming. At the same time, bright red lights on the control board began flashing on and off.

It was a hot, stuffy summer evening. The guard at the control board was almost asleep, but the alarm made him spring into action. He flicked off the alarm system. A check of the red lights showed that someone had opened the vault door at the Purolator armored car headquarters.

Checking that his gun was loaded, the guard dashed to his car. He drove at top speed to the Purolator office. Nothing suspicious on the outside, he noted. He ran up to the door with his gun drawn and rang the bell. After a minute, the guard, Ralph Marrera, opened the door, a half-filled cup of coffee in his hand.

"What's up?" Ralph asked.

"Are you kidding?" the man from Wells Fargo asked in disbelief. "Someone's in your vault!"

Together the two men dodged around the parked armored cars to reach the vault at the back. They slowed down and carefully kept behind cover as they approached the vault, but the door was locked! There was no sign that anything at all was wrong.

The two guards checked around the vault and saw no sign that anyone had been there. "Probably a short circuit," said Ralph. The Wells Fargo guard agreed. He started to fill out the reports he had to file for a false alarm.

About three hours later, the exact same thing happened. The alarm started sounding at Wells Fargo. Again the Wells Fargo guard sped over to Purolator. And once more a careful check showed that nothing had been disturbed. Ralph said he would tell the officials in the morning to have the electrical system checked out.

Over the next few weeks, the alarm was

triggered several more times. Each time the Wells Fargo guard came right over. Then, early in October 1974, the alarm sounded still another time. Suspecting a false alarm, the Wells Fargo guard just called Purolator on the telephone. He asked Ralph to check the vault. Ralph said that everything was fine. The guard just listed it as an electrical failure, without even bothering to go over.

That was the moment Charlie Marzano was waiting for. Charlie, a truck driver who had been in trouble with the law several times over the years, had come up with this absolutely wild scheme to rob Purolator. It was a plan as brilliant as it was simple.

First he enlisted the help of his friend Ralph Marrera, who worked as a guard at Purolator. He told Ralph to volunteer to work weekend nights—the time when no one else was in the office. The vault, though, was filled with many millions of dollars waiting to be taken to the bank on Monday.

Then one evening Charlie and Ralph went through the desk of the Purolator official who opened and locked the vault every day. They found the combination of the vault lock written on a slip of paper. Charlie copied the numbers and returned the paper.

While Ralph was getting ready within the Purolator office, Charlie was assembling a gang for the job. Most of the men had legitimate jobs, but they were all willing to pick up some extra cash, even by dishonest means.

Pete Gushi was the shrewd operator who

helped pull things together. Louis DeFonzo knew more ways to hide, transport, and invest stolen money than anyone else. James Maniatis, "Jimmy the Greek" as he was called, supplied the van for the actual robbery. And finally Tony Marzano, Charlie's cousin, helped Charlie carry out the 700 pounds of money after the robbery.

Charlie chose Sunday evening, October 20, 1974, at 8 P.M. as the time to pull off the job. Ralph opened the vault door. The alarm rang, and the Wells Fargo man called. "Everything's okay," Ralph said on the phone. When Ralph was sure that the coast was clear, he opened the garage doors. Charlie drove the drab green van into the building. Ralph then opened the door to the vault room. He propped the foot-thick door open with his flashlight.

Charlie and Tony entered the fifteen-foot-high vault. Piled high on all sides were heaps of heavy canvas bags and stacks of metal trunks. Each was crammed full of thousands of dollars of unmarked bills. The two men put on surgical gloves. Charlie cut open the bags of money, while Tony transferred the bills into the canvas duffle bags they had brought with them.

They worked as hard and fast as they could for about an hour. Their arms ached and their faces were dripping with perspiration. At one point, Tony pulled off his gloves and started to work without them, but Charlie made him put them back on. At the end of the hour, Charlie insisted that they stop, even though there were many money bags left. The duffle bags were almost too heavy to carry. Dragging them along the floor, the two men managed somehow to get them out of the vault and into the van.

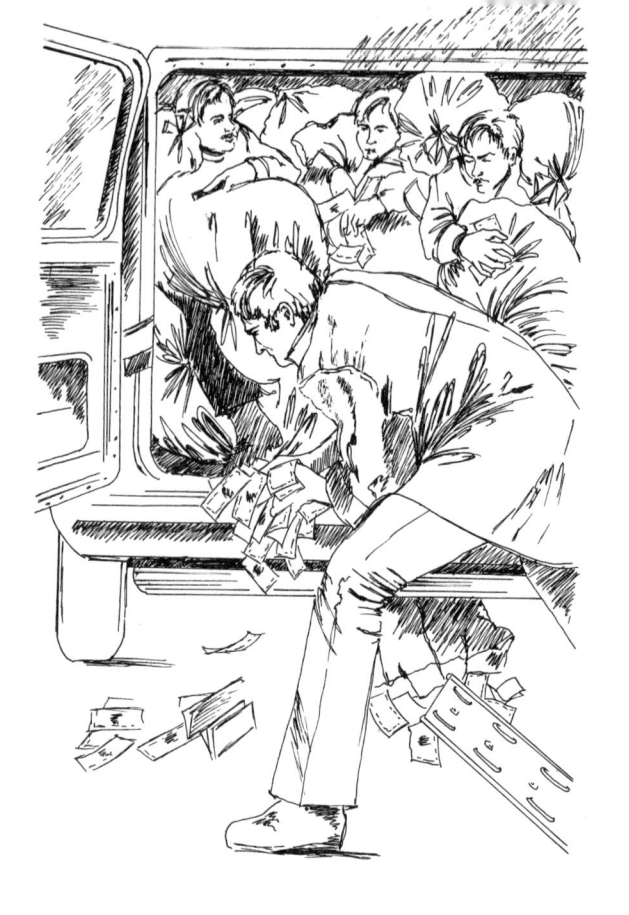

The last step before leaving was to set the vault afire. Charlie figured this would make it a case for the fire department, not the police. When they arrived they had brought in twelve plastic containers of gasoline. Now they lit a waxed cotton wick that ran to the twelve containers. Then they slammed the vault door shut and fled. What they did not realize was that the fire would soon go out in the airtight room. It would not cause any damage. This was to be the first of many mistakes.

After counting the money, $4.3 million, and hiding about half in Chicago, Charlie, Tony, Pete, and Louie, loaded the rest into a rented car and drove to Columbus, Ohio. There Louie arranged for a private plane to fly them to Grand Cayman, a Caribbean island. Grand Cayman's strict secrecy laws prevent banks from giving out information on their accounts. The reckless four paid for the flight with forty-six $100 bills. At the airport, the men attracted even more attention when they insisted on loading their exceedingly heavy bags, "sporting equipment" they said, into the small plane by themselves.

As they neared Miami, the pilot told the fugitives that they would have to land there for fuel and a customs check. Not aware of this stop, and afraid of customs, they left the plane in Miami and took rooms in a modest hotel. Without thinking, they attracted a good deal of attention by staggering through the hotel lobby dragging their heavy bags.

Pete was growing very frightened. So it was decided that he should return to Chicago. Louie would go down to Grand Cayman alone to deposit the money in secret bank accounts. And Charlie and Tony would join him later.

At Grand Cayman, the customs official opened the four suitcases. Without blinking an eye, he looked at the thousands of bills crammed into the suitcases. "Anything to declare?" he said. Louie said no. The officer waved him on. In a short while, Louie had stashed the money away in several secret accounts.

After the robbery, detectives questioned Ralph

Marrera routinely. They asked if he'd be willing to take a lie detector test. He agreed. In recounting the details of Sunday night, he was shown to be lying. Two more sessions with the FBI convinced them that Ralph had played some part in the crime. "I can't take it any more," Ralph shouted at one point. "I'm never going to talk to you again!" With that, he dashed past the guards, who were so taken aback that they stood frozen in place while Ralph made his escape.

Meanwhile, on Grand Cayman, Tony was getting restless. He could find nothing to do for entertainment. He had a bad toothache, and he was worried about the guns and walkie-talkies that he had left in his parked car at the airport in Columbus, Ohio. On October 26, he left Louie and Charlie on the island and flew back to Chicago. He picked up the car and dumped the guns behind a roadside restaurant.

All the while, though, the police net was tightening around the robbers. Ralph was captured at the home of his wife's parents two days later. A couple of days after that the police moved in on Pete and Jimmy and held them for questioning about the van. Meantime, Tony heard that his fingerprint had been found on some money recovered from the robbery, and he decided to turn himself in.

Friends told Charlie and Louie of the bad turn of events in Chicago. The two men tried to book a flight from Grand Cayman to Costa Rica. When they couldn't produce proper identification at the airport, the suspicious agent called the police. Both of them were taken into custody and placed on the first plane to Miami. Upon landing, they were arrested and flown to Chicago.

The trial was held in April 1975. Ralph, who had suffered a mental breakdown in prison, was found unfit to stand trial. After some time in a mental hospital, he was released, but he remained ill for the rest of his life.

In *The Big Steal* Anthony Marzano tells of the trial's outcome. Tony got a sentence of five years, but was released on parole after serving only twenty-eight months. Pete's sentence was for three years, but he was out in fourteen months. Jimmy served eighteen months in jail. The jury found Louie not guilty. Charlie, the mastermind of the heist, was sentenced to twenty years.

Of the stolen $4.3 million, about one-fourth was found buried in the basement of Ralph's grandmother's house. Pete claimed to have been robbed of $300,000 of his $400,000 share. A check for $1.6 million came from a Grand Cayman bank to the offices of the insurance company that covered Purolator. No one knows how or why it was paid.

Over a million dollars is still missing. The whereabouts of this money remains a mystery. Just like Blackbeard the pirate, who buried his treasure on Grand Cayman, Charlie just might have hidden his money somewhere on this little tropical island.

CHAPTER NINE

Fric-Frac: Robbery on the Riviera

Most people knew Albert Spaggiari as the tall, thin, quiet, middle-aged owner of a small photography shop in the resort city of Nice on the French Riviera. Few had any idea that he was also a reckless adventurer. Spaggiari had served time in prison, was active in extremist right-wing groups, and had a passion for excitement and easy money.

One day in September 1974, Spaggiari walked

into the large, imposing offices of Nice's Société Générale Bank to rent a safe-deposit box for his valuables and important papers. The guard led him downstairs. Together they walked past the thirty-ton door and entered the vault. Seven large metal cabinets containing thousands of safe-deposit boxes lined the walls. As Spaggiari's eyes took in the box-filled room, his mind pictured the millions of francs worth of gold, jewely, and cash stored there.

From that moment, Spaggiari began to form the notion of robbing the vault. Part of his inspiration came from the desire to be incredibly rich. The rest came from a yearning to take risks and live dangerously outside the law. By the time he left the bank, a plan for *le fric-frac du siecle,* the bank robbery of the century, was in place. Bit by bit he worked out the steps of an ingenious scheme. In *The Gentlemen of 16 July* René Louis Maurice and Ken Follett give the details of this exciting crime.

The first part involved learning more about the bank and its vault. Each time Spaggiari went down to use his own safe-deposit box, he took measurements of the vault. He made drawings to scale of the bank's floor plan. He even took photos with a miniature camera. Spaggiari gathered a lot of additional information from a teller he befriended. And he picked up the latest gossip from bank workers who took coffee at the cafe across the street.

The smooth-talking Spaggiari also enlisted the help of Charlotte, a seventy-eight-year-old woman who had a safe-deposit box at the same bank tending to be worried about her money asked the guard all sorts of questions about the security system. Then she passed the answers along to Spaggiari. From Charlotte, Spaggiari learned that the bank had no monitoring system. Only three out of the four walls of the vault were wired with alarms. And no guards kept watch at night.

Thanks to a little trick of his own, Spaggiari was able to convince himself that the vault had no alarm system. One afternoon he placed an alarm clock, with an especially loud ring, into his safe-deposit box. He set the clock to go off at midnight, and waited at the cafe across from the bank. If the vault was wired for sound, he figured, the ear-shattering ring would trigger an alarm. He would see the police arriving. But nothing happened. The next day he checked his box. The alarm part was all wound down. This proved that it had sounded, but had not been heard.

At this point, Spaggiari began to work on the second part of of the plan—how to get into the bank. Spaggiari picked up this information quite accidentally. He overheard someone say that the city's sewers were situated around the bank. So he got a map of the sewer lines from town hall. He saw that they passed within four or five yards of the wall of the vault. It happened to be the wall that Spaggiari knew was not wired. The map even showed the location of the manholes that led down into the sewer from the street level.

Soon Spaggiari's basic plan for entering Nice's biggest bank was set: He would follow the sewer line to the point closest to the vault wall. Then he would tunnel from the sewer pipe to the vault wall. Finally, he would break through the wall, get into the vault, open all the boxes, and escape through the sewers. Now all that Spaggiari needed was a gang to help him carry out the plan.

It was early 1976 before Spaggiari had put together his group of eighteen men. About half were friends he could trust and experts who could handle some of the difficult tasks that had to be done. The rest were crooks and hoodlums from France's nearby city of Marseilles. For the most part, the members of the two gangs knew each other by nickname only.

Spaggiari's next job was to obtain the equipment that was needed. The group fanned out through the Riviera and other parts of France, buying or stealing tools and supplies for the heist. The list seemed to go on forever: axes and shovels for digging, blow torches and oxygen cylinders to blast open the strongbox doors, pipes to vent the smoke and heat of the torches, wires to bring electricity into the sewers, cars and trucks to get to and from the job, two rubber dinghies to transport equipment through the sewer pipes, flashlights, food and drink, first-aid kits. As the supplies came in, Spaggiari stored them in a vacant villa a few miles from Nice.

On April 7, 1976, the Sewer Rats, as they came to be called, were ready. At 9:45 that evening, Spaggiari and three others were dressed as sewer workers. They stopped their small truck near a manhole cover in the middle of the street. Two of the men jumped out of the van and set up a "Men Working" sign over the manhole. Another pried off the heavy metal lid. Spaggiari and Pierre, head of the Marseilles group, went down the ladder. Leaving the two men there for the night, the van driver pulled the cover back over the manhole, removed the sign, and drove away.

For the next seven hours, Spaggiari and Pierre moved through the four-foot-high, three-foot-wide, slime-covered sewage pipe. They had only a little light from their flashlights to cut through the darkness. As they waded through the two-foot-high stream of raw, stinking sewage, they were sometimes struck on the head by fresh sewage from pipes above them. They also had to dodge the huge rats that darted around. Gagging, wheezing, and panting, they nevertheless managed to locate the tunnel that ran close to the bank. They found their way back to the manhole before daybreak, where their pals were waiting to whisk them back to their hideout.

For the next week, they followed the same routine. All day they slept; all night they explored the sewers. By the end of seven days, the surveying was done. The maps were ready. The men knew the sewer route like the backs of their hands.

Spaggiari ordered the big push to begin on May 8, 1976. The gang members dropped into the sewer from the back of the truck one by one. Loaded down like pack mules with drills, hammers, and chisels, they trudged through the muck to reach the right spot. Then, with a jackknife, Spaggiari outlined a rectangle thirty-six inches by twenty-nine inches on the sewer wall. That was where they should drill to get closest to the bank wall.

After several nights (they couldn't work during the day for fear of being seen or heard), they had a hole large enough for a man to crawl through. The next hurdle was to dig a tunnel from the sewer line to the bank wall—a distance of some twenty-five feet through earth and solid rock. Every inch of the way was hard going. Drilling through the rock was especially slow, noisy, and messy.

By now it was May 27. They had been digging for nearly three weeks. Spaggiari was the first to see the foundation wall of the bank. It was five feet thick and made of heavy stones embedded in reinforced concrete. The men attacked it with their drills. Work time was limited to the few hours of night when watchmen, cleaning people, or pedestrians were not around. One time, the men spent a whole night in the tunnel—but could only chip away at the wall for three hours.

The work was going very slowly. So Spaggiari decided to bring down two electric drills. That meant lugging another 330 pounds of equipment through the sewers. They also needed 500 yards of waterproof wire to hook up to an outlet in a nearby underground garage. But the idea worked. The electric drills quickly pierced the bank wall. By the next day they had a man-sized opening.

Now they were ready to begin work on the vault itself. With a powerful hydraulic jack, the giant steel box was tilted up far enough to let a man slip in underneath. Spaggiari and Pierre tossed a coin to see who would go first. It was heads. Pierre slipped through the narrow gap. Spaggiari followed a second later. They were inside the bank. It was 9:30 P.M., Friday, July 16. They had until early Monday morning to empty out the safe-deposit boxes.

With blow torches and crowbars they got to work. The torches made it very hot in the airless room. And it was very slow going. After eighteen hours they had only opened twenty-eight boxes. The men were very disappointed. These boxes were mostly filled with stocks and bonds. They held very few jewels and hardly any cash.

The thieves bettered their technique. It took only six hours for them to open another twenty-eight boxes. Also, their luck improved. Now they began finding gold, diamonds, coins, and bills in all denominations. Bags of money rained down on them as cash receipts from supermarkets and department stores were placed in a night-deposit chute that emptied into the vault. They gathered an estimated 10 million francs that way.

At 1:04 A.M., Monday, July 19, Spaggiari said that it was time to leave. Loaded with riches, the thieves donned their street clothes and formed a human chain to move the loot from the vault to the tunnel. Some of the treasure was put into backpacks weighing up to 120 pounds. The rest was moved through the filthy sewers on rubber dinghies. Five hours later, everything was packed into trucks. The gang members made a safe getaway with their haul—about 60 million francs ($12.4 million)!

All Nice was up in arms when the news of the bank heist hit the streets. A huge police investigation was launched at once. The gang had left very few clues behind. No fingerprints. No source of supply of materials. No witnesses.

Eventually, the hideout was located. People came forward who had seen the men moving in and out of the house. Some forty suspects were arrested. Among them were two who confessed to the crime. Under questioning, they named Spaggiari as the mastermind behind the heist.

Spaggiari was picked up in Nice without any struggle. He was accused of the crime and jailed. And it is here that the story takes a bizarre twist, even stranger than the robbery itself.

On March 10, 1977, Spaggiari was being questioned by a judge. Suddenly, he stood up, dashed to the window, and leaped out. Landing first on a door ledge, he then jumped down to the roof of a parked car. One more bound and he was on the ground. A motorcycle was waiting with its engine roaring. Throwing a leg over the seat, Spaggiari was whisked away in a cloud of exhaust.

A moment later, motorcycle and passenger whipped into the garage of an apartment house. Spaggiari dove into a hiding spot created under the back seat of a large British car. The car pulled out of the garage at a dignified five miles per hour. As police and cars wildly zipped by, the car slowly made its way from Nice to Paris. It was stopped and searched fourteen times. But no one ever thought to look under the back seat.

Through underground connections, two French reporters later tracked Spaggiari to Madrid, Spain. It is here that he is believed to be living today in safety and comfort. Late in 1982, a bank at the Spanish resort of Marbella was robbed of about $16 million. Witnesses reported seeing Spaggiari in the vicinity.

Could the mastermind of the century's greatest *fric-frac* have struck again?

CHAPTER TEN

Mel Weinberg: The King of Con

Con men, short for confidence men, are often the smartest and most charming members of the underworld. Their success is based on gaining the trust of their victims, or marks. Then they swindle them in con games, or scams. Usually the scams are set up so that the marks can't go to the police without getting into trouble themselves. Of all the con men in America, probably the cleverest and most successful is Mel Weinberg, the "King of Con."

According to Robert W. Greene in *The Sting Man,* Mel began his career very early, in 1931, at the age of six! He was in first grade in the Bronx, New York City. Whenever the teacher's back was turned, Mel would swipe a few gold stars from her desk. When he brought them home, his mother thought he had earned them. She was very proud of her little boy.

The day of reckoning came on the last day of school. Mel brought his mother the news that he was not being promoted The shocked woman went to speak to the teacher the very next day.

"How could you fail a student who brings home gold stars every day?" she asked.

The teacher hesitated before she replied. "If Melvin is bringing home gold stars, you can be sure they are not ones that *I* gave him."

Thus, Mel's first scam ended in failure, but he said it taught him two important lessons. "Always have a good excuse. And always split the scene if you see two of your marks getting together."

Not surprisingly, Mel Weinberg dropped out of school in the eighth grade. During World War II he served in the navy. After discharge he took a job in his father's glass business. However, he was not earning very much until he met an official of the glazier's union.

The official offered to pay Weinberg for breaking the windows of stores not hiring union glass workers. Using a slingshot to send metal bolts through storefronts, Mel kept his part of the deal. The payments from the union leader gave Mel the extra money he wanted. The increased demand for replacement panes gave a lift to his father's business as well.

Nevertheless, Mel didn't see any future in glass. He decided to seek his fortune in California. Soon after his arrival, he heard of a manufacturer who had mistakenly produced thousands of pairs of socks without the foot part. Alert to an opportunity for a good con, Mel offered to buy all 5,000 pairs at ten cents per hundred—provided he got the same number of regular labels. The deal was struck, and Weinberg took the socks home. He pasted on the labels and tied the socks into bundles of six, carefully hiding the missing part.

Mel then sold the socks at factory gates—six pair for a dollar. He was sure never to go to the same factory twice. If a customer wanted to open a bundle, Mel would whisper, "There's a cop over there," and scamper away.

By the time the sock supply was exhausted, Mel was ready to return to New York. It was there, around 1970, that he started the scam operation that established his reputation as the top con man of his time. He repeated the same scam hundreds of times.

The scheme, which worked so well, started as Weinberg spread the word that he had connections at foreign banks. He called himself Swiss Bank Associates, and let it be known that his banks had cash to lend to business people with poor credit ratings or those who could not borrow from anyone else.

In a short while, his business started to boom. A typical case might involve a real-estate investor. Suppose this man wants to borrow money in a hurry. From a friend in a mayor's office he has learned that a city is planning to build a road in an undeveloped area. The road will open up a new part of the city. Real-estate values will skyrocket. A plot of 200 acres now sells for $2 million. It will be worth about five times that much once the road is built.

The investor wants to buy the land before the price goes up, but he can't raise that much cash. And he is reluctant to go to his local bank. He doesn't want them to know about the road. If word leaks out, it will ruin his chance to make a fortune.

The investor is what Mel calls a DM (Desperate Man), a perfect mark for his scam. When the DM calls, Weinberg invites him out to his very posh Long Island office. He even offers the man the use of his chauffeur-driven limousine to get him there. The chauffeur, though, is coached on what questions to ask the investor about his business, and what answers to give about Mel's success in arranging loans. All this is recorded. Mel makes sure he listens to the tape before he sees the client.

The office itself is also designed to impress the DM. Signed photos of leading politicians line the walls. The glowing inscriptions—all forged—stand out impressively. Furnished tastefully, at a cost of over $70,000, the office gives the impression of great wealth.

As though he were a bank officer granting a loan, Mel questions the investor very carefully. He examines the man's financial statements. Finally, he fakes putting through a phone call to Europe, and gives the investor the answer he is hoping for. Weinberg's overseas bank will grant the loan —on receipt of the financial report and loan application. However, before the delighted investor departs, Mel makes one small request. He asks for $5,000—the up-front fee, to be paid in advance for processing the application. The client may hesitate a moment at this point. But so tempting is the potential profit that he usually gives Mel the money.

The next part of the scam is known as the stall. Mel offers the anxious client dozens of reasons for the delay in getting the loan approval: warfare in the Middle East, a rail strike in Europe, computer failure, death of a bank officer, a terrorist attack, upcoming elections. His guidelines are simple: Tell the truth except when you absolutely must lie. And always hold out hope for the mark.

When Mel can stall the investor no longer, he forges a letter from the bank. It says that the DM's loan has been refused. Of course, the borrower is out $5,000. But for another $5,000 fee, Mel says, he can try for the loan in a different way. The added fee will get the mark forged papers showing that he has a large sum of money on deposit in another overseas bank. With that as security, Weinberg assures him, there will be no trouble in getting the loan approved.

Most investors produce still another $5,000 fee for Weinberg at this point. Again Mel stalls as long as he can. Finally, he produces a letter of rejection. The client has now spent $10,000, and hasn't received a thing, but there is nothng he can do. He has no contract and no written proof of Weinberg's promises. And he is also guilty of having used the forged deposit statement.

Before long, Weinberg's up-front scam was netting him about a million dollars a year. During those years, whenever he came across information that would be helpful to the FBI, and not harmful to him, he passed them the tip. Some day, he figured, he might want a favor from the FBI. It would be wise to stay on their good side.

Actually, the opposite happened. The FBI turned to Mel for help. In 1977 FBI agents asked Weinberg for assistance in their work against "white-collar" crime. These are crimes in which money is stolen, not with guns and force, but by swindles, extortion, fraud, and other nonviolent means. Mel agreed to cooperate. And this led to the most famous scam of all, known as Abscam, short for Abdul scam.

Abscam's first targets were dishonest business people. However, it soon set its sights on bribe-taking government officials—ranging from small-town politicians to members of Congress. In this scam, Weinberg claimed to represent a wealthy Arab sheik, Abdul. Abdul was willing to pay thousands of dollars in bribes for special favors from various government officials. Between Weinberg's skill as a con man, and the greed for Abdul's oil money, the FBI was very successful. They were able to indict one United States senator, six representatives, and a long list of lesser officials for bribery and other crimes.

After testifying at the Abscam trials, Mel Weinberg disappeared. No one knows where he went. Abscam had made him too well known. And his earlier scams had made him the target of many marks seeking revenge.

However, most people doubt that Mel Weinberg is really out of circulation. At this moment, he is probably working some new con game on some unsuspecting mark.

BIBLIOGRAPHY

The following books give specific details about the crimes in this book:

Behn, Noel. *The Big Stick-Up at Brinks* (Tony Pino). New York: G. P. Putnam's, 1977.

Bloom, Murray Teigh. *The Man Who Stole Portugal* (Alves Reis). New York: Charles Scribner's, 1966.

Green, A. C. *The Santa Claus Bank Robbery* (Santa Claus). New York: Alfred Knopf, 1972.

Greene, Robert W. *The Sting Man* (Mel Weinberg). New York: Ballantine Books, 1981.

Marzano, Anthony. *The Big Steal* (Charlie Marzano). Boston: Houghton Mifflin, 1980.

Maurice, René Louis and Ken Follett. *The Gentlemen of 16 July* (Albert Spaggiari). New York: Arbor House, 1978.

Read, Piers Paul. *The Train Robbers* (Ronald Biggs). Philadelphia: Lippincott, 1978.

Reit, Seymour V. *The Day They Stole the Mona Lisa* (Vincenzo Perugia). New York: Summit Books, 1981.

Spaggiari, Albert. *Fric-Frac* (Albert Spaggiari). Boston: Houghton Mifflin, 1979.

Swanberg, W. A. *The Rector and the Rogue* (Gentleman Joe). New York: Charles Scribner's, 1968.

Wallace, Edgar. *Stranger than Fiction* (Martin Guerre). New York: Howell, Soskin, 1947.

The following books include accounts of several other bizarre crimes:

Adams, Laurie. *Art Cop.* New York: Dodd, Mead, 1974.

Gribble, Leonard. *Famous Mysteries of Modern Times.* London: Muller, 1976.

Hyde, H. Montgomery. *An International Casebook of Crime.* London: Barrie and Rockliff, 1962.

Keating, H. R. F. *Great Crimes.* New York: Harmony, 1982.

Luisi, Gerard and Charles Samuels. *How to Catch 5000 Thieves.* New York: Macmillan, 1962.

Nash, Jay Robert. *Hustlers and Con Men.* New York: Evans, 1976.

Phelan, James. *Scandals, Scamps and Scoundrels.* New York: Random House, 1982.

Rosberg, Robert R. *Game of Thieves.* New York: Everest House, 1980.

Tidyman, Ernest. *Big Bucks.* New York: Norton, 1982.

Index

Abscam, 91
Alarm systems, 56, 68–70, 78
Angola, 38, 41, 43
Armored car robberies, 53–60, 68–75
Art crimes, 7, 10–11, 29–36
Artigat, France, 13, 15–19

Bandeira, Jośe, 38
Bank accounts, 40, 73
Bank crimes, 7, 38–41, 44–52, 76–84, 87
Bank of Angola & Metrople, 40, 41
Bank of Portugal, 38, 40–42
Bertrande (wife of Martin Guerre), 13–19
Biggs, Ronald, 62, 66–67
Big Steal, The (Marzano), 75
Blackmail, 24
Bodies, stolen, 8
Boles, Charles E. (Black Bart), 9, 10
Boston, Brinks holdup in, 53–60
Brazil, 66–67
Bredius, Dr., 10
Bribes, 43, 91
Brinks holdup, Boston, 53–60
Byrnes, Captain Thomas, 24, 26, 27

Carmona, General Oscar, 43
Chaudron, Yves, 33, 34
Chicago, Purolator heist in, 68, 73–75
Cisco, Texas, 44–52
Con, 85–91
Confessions, 28, 83
Cordrey, Roger, 62, 63–65
Counterfeiting, 38, 41, 42
"The Crime of the Century." *See* Brinks holdup, Boston

Davis, Louis, 44, 48–49
DeFonzo, Louis, 71, 73–75
Dix, Reverend Dr. Morgan, 20–28
DM (Desperate Man), 89

Edwards, Buster, 62
Electric chair, 50, 52
Escapes, 61–62
Extortion, 24, 28

Fake money, 38, 41, 42
FBI, 58, 59, 74, 90, 91
Fingerprints, 34, 74
First National Bank, Texas, 45–48
Florence, Italy, 35
Follett, Ken, 77
Forgery, 10–11, 34, 35, 38–39, 43, 89, 90

Garden City, Long Island, 8
Gayler, James, 24, 27
Gentlemen Joe. *See* Williamson, Eugene Fairfax
Gentlemen of 16 July, The (Maurice, Follett), 77
Goody, Gordon, 62
Government, 37–43, 91
Grand Cayman (island), 73, 74, 75
Greene, Robert W., 86
Guerre, Martin, 13–19
Guerre, Pierre, 15, 16
Gushi, Pete, 70, 73, 74, 75

Hanging, 19, 52
Helms, Henry, 44, 48–52
Hennies, Adolf, 38
Hill, Robert, 44, 48–52
Hirasawa, Sadamichi, 7

—
94

Impersonation, 7, 13–19, 30–32, 91
Informers, 53, 60
Investigation leads, 26–29, 34, 41, 53, 59–60, 65, 83

Kidnappings, 48, 67
"King of Con." *See* Weinberg, Mel

Lancelotti, Michele, 39–36
Lancelotti, Vincent, 30–36
Leads, investigation, 26–29, 34, 41, 53, 59–60, 65, 83
Louvre Museum, Paris, 29–36

Manhunts, 50, 58
Maniatis, James, 71, 74, 75
Marang, Karl, 38, 39
Marrera, Ralph, 69–71, 74–75
Marzano, Charlie, 68, 70–75
Marzano, Tony, 71–75
Maurice, René Louis, 77
Meegeren, Hans Van, 10–11
Mona Lisa, theft of, 29–36
Motive, criminal, 7, 10, 15, 28, 33, 35, 38, 40, 77
Museum theft, 29–36

Newspapers, 24, 25, 41
Nice, France, 77–84

O'Keefe, Specs, 60

Paintings, 10, 11, 30–36
Paris, France, 29–36
Parole, 54
Perugia, Vincenzo, 29–36
Peters, Samuel T., 25, 26
Pino, Tony, 53–60
Plagiarism, 28
Portugal, Reis affair in, 37–43
Prosecution, criminal, 11, 19, 28, 36, 37, 43, 50, 60, 65, 75
Purolator Heist, Chicago, 68–75

Ransom money, 8, 24
Ratliff, Marshall, 44, 45, 48–52
Reis, Alves, 37–43

Revenge, 10, 60, 91
Rewards, 34, 45, 47
Robberies. *See specific types of robberies*
Rosenbaum, Adolph, 26

Salazar, Antonio, 43
Santa Claus robbery, 44–52
Scams, 15, 20–28, 33, 35, 38–43, 85–91
Scotland Yard, 65
Sentences, criminal, 11, 19, 28, 36, 37, 43, 50, 60, 65, 75
Sewer Rats, 79
Société Générale Bank robbery, Nice, France, 77–84
Spaggiari, Albert, 76–84
Stagecoach robberies, 8, 9
Stall, 89
Stewart, Alexander T., 7, 8
Sting Man, The (Greene), 86

Teikdsu Bank, Tokyo, 7
Train robberies, 60–67
Trinity Parish, New York City, 20–28

Valfierno, Eduardo de, 33–36
Vermeer, Jan, 10–11

Wandsworth Prison, England, 61, 66
Waterlow, Sir William, 39
Weinberg, Mel, 85–91
Wells Fargo Security, Chicago, 68
Williamson, Eugene Fairfax (Gentleman Joe), 20–28
Witnesses, 11, 17, 18

95

About the Authors

In this volume Gilda and Melvin Berger bring together a number of accounts of the most intriguing crimes from their files of undercover and illegal activities. Working together and separately, the Bergers have over ninety books to their credit. Many have won special recognition by the Library of Congress, the New York Public Library, the Child Study Association, and the Children's Book Council. In addition, their books have been widely translated, and excerpts appear in a number of anthologies. The authors live and work in Great Neck, New York, devoting full time to writing books for young people.